RIDINGS HIGH

Also available in this series:

Fred Archer	BENEDICT'S POOL
Peter Austen	THE COUNTRY ANTIQUE DEALER
Mary Barnard	THE DIARY OF AN OPTIMIST
Pip Beck	A WAAF IN BOMBER COMMAND
Adrian Bell	THE CHERRY TREE
Mary Sydney Burke	THE SOLDIER'S WIFE
Jennifer Davies	TALES OF THE OLD GYPSIES
Roger Hutchings	CRYSTAL PALACE VISTAS
Ken Hankins	A CHILD OF THE THIRTIES
Herbert C. Harrison	THE MILL HOUSE AND THEREABOUTS
Gregory Holyoake	THE PREFAB KID
Erma Harvey James	WITH MAGIC IN MY EYES
Joy Lakeman	THEM DAYS
Len Langrick	SNOWBALL: GO FIND YOURSELF A SCHOOL
Florence Mary McDowell	OTHER DAYS AROUND ME
Madeline MacDonald	THE LAST YEAR OF THE GANG
Angela Mack	DANCING ON THE WAVES
Brian P. Martin	TALES FROM THE COUNTRY PUB
Roger Mason	GRANNY'S VILLAGE
Cicely Mayhew	BEADS ON A STRING
Christian Miller	A CHILDHOOD IN SCOTLAND
Katharine Moore	QUEEN VICTORIA IS VERY ILL
J. C. Morten	I REMAIN, YOUR SON JACK
and Sheila Morten	
Pauline Neville	PEGGY
Humphrey Phelps	JUST ACROSS THE FIELDS
Angela Raby	THE FORGOTTEN SERVICE
Phyl Surman	PRIDE OF THE MORNING
Doreen Louie West	LOUIE: AN OXFORD LADY
Elizabeth West	HOVEL IN THE HILLS
Hazel Wheeler	HALF A POUND OF TUPPENNY RICE
William Woodrow	ANOTHER TIME, ANOTHER PLACE

Ridings High

William Woodrow

ISIS
LARGE PRINT
Oxford

First published in Great Britain 2002
by ISIS Publishing Ltd

Published in Large Print 2002 by ISIS Publishing Ltd,
7 Centremead, Osney Mead, Oxford OX2 0ES
by arrangement with William Woodrow

British Library Cataloguing in Publication Data
Woodrow, William
  Ridings high. – Large print ed. – (Isis reminiscence series)
  1. Woodrow, William 2. Country life – England –
  Yorkshire Dales 3. Large type books 4. Yorkshire Dales
  (England) – Biography
  I. Title
  942.8'4'082'0922

ISBN 0-7531-9726-X (hb)
ISBN 0-7531-9727-8 (pb)

Printed and bound by Antony Rowe, Chippenham and Reading

Preface

James Joyce once said — I think it was to Sylvia Beach, who first published *Ulysses* — that he was better able to focus upon the city of Dublin when in exile than if he had stayed put in the place of his birth.

To equate myself with Joyce in any other way than sharing this characteristic is preposterous: unthinkable. But I could never have written about Yorkshire with the same mixture of affection and exasperation if we had not moved south on retirement to be nearer the grandchildren in the Midlands.

My wife, though Yorkshire through and through, found the move no hardship. She has inherited the nomadic tendencies of her paternal grandfather. For myself I felt the move to be hurtful and at times intolerable. A deep resentment clouded my mind at the thought that I could no longer return to the places I loved except as a visitor; a tourist.

My wife had no feelings of this kind: or if she did, she disguised them well. By her reasoning our separate feelings were the natural outcome of the fact that she was a native, I was an off comed un-even though my stay was some thirty years. Being Yorkshire born, she reasoned, it did not matter where we lived she would always carry Yorkshire with her in her mind.

We go back, quite often: but not often enough for me. We visit much loved places in the Huddersfield, Brighouse and Colne Valley area: but it's not the same. We take the once familiar road through Keighley and Skipton to the Dales. But beyond Skipton the road has been "straightened", by-passes built and the old sense of travelling home is only slightly stirred by the sight of the once familiar orange and black Pennine buses.

We arrive in Settle — once our nearest town. We park in the large car park just off the town centre. Once we were at home there; now just two who mingle anonymously with the coach party who are on some kind of tour — Skipton to Settle to Kendal and thence to Blackpool for a night out.

It is then that it hurts most — the feeling of not belonging any more. We simply look at Pen-y-ghent, at Ingleborough. We look across from Buckhaw Brow to Giggleswick School where my wife taught music in the late fifties and early sixties. How could we ever have left the place? But we did and we had persuasive reason for doing so.

Greatly moved we make a futile round of the local estate agents and study their offers — for old times sake — in the "Naked Man" café. And all this happens time and again: not just once.

Our visits always end in the same way. Reluctant to retrace our steps we strike out westward for the M6 and as we make the return journey to the Midlands we remind each other that we went on the first bit of the M6 to be opened to the public, near Lancaster, on the day that it opened.

Last year's visit was no different from many others except in one particular. I was making my resentment vocal with more vehemence than usual when my wife interrupted my diatribe.

"If you feel so strongly about it you know what you ought to do, don't you?"

"Go on, what?"

"Write a book about the place."

And here it is.

Introduction

Although I lived there for nearly thirty years, and love the place enough to yearn to be back once more, I am still reminded, when I become nostalgic, that there is no such thing as an "adopted Yorkshireman". You are either Yorkshire or you are not. To use the vernacular, either summat or nowt. There are no half measures.

I am constantly reminded of this by a spouse of getting on for 50 years duration, who unequivocally IS Yorkshire. So much so that she regards Derbyshire as a suburb of Sheffield.

It is simplistic to say that a Yorkshire person is one who was born within certain geographical parameters. That is a necessary pre-requisite certainly, but not the only qualifying factor. Being called Sykes or Crowther or Sutcliffe (or in contemporary vein Patel or Mohammed) do not, in themselves, hold out much hope of vicarious membership of that most select nation called "Yorkshire Folk". These are all superficial trimmings and count for little. To take the matter further, not everyone born in Yorkshire qualifies either: Yorkshireness is an indefinable, almost an occult, quality; only another Yorkshire person can say definitively "tha's reet". It is the equivalent of being dubbed with a regal sword.

Because it is such a vast and sprawling place it is not possible to capture the spirit (or essence) of Yorkshire in a page or two. It has to do with geography and geology on the one hand and human history on the other. This book is neither earth science nor history in the wider sense. It is a book of reminiscences, a tapestry of memories that will satisfy my nostalgic urges on the one hand, and — maybe — create in the mind of a reader a train of thought that begins with "Yes, that once happened to me . . . I remember . . ." And from that stimulus another book may be born. For this reason, then, I feel that it is appropriate to begin with a simple topographical tour of the region in which I have spent almost a third of my life so far. I had the good fortune to live in a wide range of places from high up in the Pennines, surrounded by mountains and fells, to a village on the very edge of what used to be called the "heavy woollen district" but which is now better known as the *Last of the Summer Wine* country.

The beauty of landscape, like the enduring beauty of women, may be attributed to bone structure. The bones of landscape are the underlying rocks of the earth. The composition and structure of these rocks give us the multifarious landscape features that may be seen on a journey through Yorkshire.

There are the wild upland reaches of the Northern Dales with their sombre and treeless acres of peat and heather moor. These are some of the remotest and most uncompromising country in Britain. Here the

5

curlew blends his evocative cries with the more strident call of the grouse. The mountain hares turn white in winter just like their Arctic counterparts elsewhere. More than this, on the crag behind our house, a pair of ravens nested. We were too close to its base to see Ingleborough, but we had a glorious view of Pen-y-ghent — at all seasons and in all weathers. This was Pennine gritstone country. Further south lies the lighter, brighter and, to some eyes, the less dramatic limestone country. With its threadbare look of exposed rocks thrusting up through short and springy turf. This is the land of caves and caverns, pothole and underground streams; where dry valleys and steep gorges owe their existence to the solubility of the rock in the slightly acid rain. Gritstone or limestone, whichever, it is all a great joy to me, not least because it can be summed up in farming terms as "sheep country": and I love sheep.

Not for nothing is this called Carboniferous limestone. Associated with the limestone, above it but dipping away beneath other strata are the coal measures. These, along with the formidable Millstone grit, various layers of sandstones and shales lie one above another like a crooked pile of assorted sandwiches on a plate: in this case a plate of Silurian shale. It is hard to imagine that these wild and, to some, inhospitable, uplands were once alive with industry. Not only coal but iron and lead and tin are found here and each has left its mark on the landscape through the hands of men who worked the mines since prehistoric times. Even today traces of their one-time presence remain in a most unlikely place. On the plateau that is the summit of Ingleborough there is evidence of a one-time race track. Long ago the pitmen from the villages of Ingleton and Clapham would take their ponies up Ingleborough and race them. Those are the facts: imagination will embroider them at will to make a story or even a legend. And like all remote and mountainous regions mysteries and legends abound and some of them will be told in other parts of this book.

From Yorkshire's northern boundary, sweeping away southwards and fanning out to around twenty miles in the south are the Vales of Mowbray and York. This is gentler and more submissive landscape, farmed with equal success by arable and livestock farmers and, significantly, the home of several important studs and racing stables. We lived for a time on the edge of this area but we were never so much involved in it as we were in the high Pennines.

Despite its softness, the bone structure is here too of course. But it is buried deep under deposits of fertile clay and drift. This was left behind by the retreating ice-sheets of the Ice Age more than 12,000 years ago. In geological terms, of course, this is no more than the merest tick in time. These same ice-sheets also melted to form a vast inland sea, the waters dammed in by the rock rubble and debris that formed a natural barrier. Much later the waters escaped and left behind a soft and friable soil that is exceedingly fertile. The Vale of Pickering was recently inundated once again by flood waters returning to reclaim their heritage.

Also young in the geological sense are the Wolds: one of the richest arable farmlands in the country. Here the obvious prosperity and efficiency of the farming gives the lie to the original Saxon meaning of "Wold: an open tract of uncultivated land". The Wolds are chalklands but the further east you go the more the chalk is buried beneath the peaty deposits and glacial debris of Holderness.

North Humberside (still called East Riding in the county itself) reminds me of east Anglia. It is a balance of land and sky. It has a seaboard and it specialises in growing sugarbeet and grain. The similarity to East Anglia increases as you look at the place names: Swinefleet, Skidby, North Ferriby, Eastrington and the like are all Norse and Saxon in origin. This region is not to everyone's taste. Even Chaucer saw only its bleakest aspects and he wrote: "Lordinges, ther is in Yorkshire as I guess, a marshy contree called Holderness".

This, then is the skeleton: the framework upon which Nature has laid the flesh and Man the clothing. I could go on deepening and broadening this sweep of landscape but this is a collection of memories: of people and places. It is not a textbook of environmental science, although I have often been tempted to write one. It is remembrances of the world as it was, as I enjoyed it from the late fifties to the mid-eighties. Much has now changed. The landscapes that I loved and lived in were secret places thirty and more years ago. Now, largely thanks to television, they have been invaded and are marketed as "Herriot Country",

Last of the Summer Wine country, *Heartbeat* Country and the rest. They are visited annually by thousands of trippers and sightseers. Most of my Yorkshire years were spent in one or another of these "tele-countries". What I saw and knew and grew to love may still be found there; if you know where to look.

Because I respect the privacy and peace that the genuine residents still enjoy I have taken liberties with names and places. All the places I describe do exist and the people written about are real people but their names have been changed. However, those who know and love the same areas that I have written about will find it easy to work out the truth behind the tales. And that is exactly as it should be.

Ashes to Ashes

Farmers, be warned! There may well be a poor harvest next year. How do I know? Folklore has it that a plentiful crop of rowan berries in any Autumn indicates a poor harvest next season.

This piece of country wisdom used to be quoted — along with other doom-laden pronouncements — by my Grandmother at least sixty years ago.

This year I have noticed a particular abundance of the berries of these most beautiful of our trees. From the pale orange to deepest crimson, clusters of berries presently adorn the rowans of city avenues and rural hedgerows alike. This is one tree which appears to be equally at home in town and country. And it is just as well for us that it is — if one is to believe even half of the old tales about the rowan (or Mountain Ash as it is called in the North).

Twigs, flowers and fruit alike are a potent force for good against the powers of darkness — so history tells us. Probing the past, we discover that those same powers of darkness are the ancient pre-Christian gods and goddesses that were fought against by the True Faith in Roman times. Druids of Celtic Britain had their trinity of oak, ash and thorn. They had the mistletoe. But against these the early Christians fought with the support of bundles of rowan twigs and coronets of rowan-berries in and out of season.

Even today, in some remote areas, farmers will hang bunches of berried twigs, bound with red ribbon, over barn doors — to keep away the powers of evil from their livestock. This is a tradition that is practised with serious intent amongst the commercialised cavortings on Halloween.

And who knows how many unsophisticated country wives and daughters still wear necklaces of dried rowan berries to ward off spells likely to be cast by the local wise woman or witch?

In more practical vein, rowan berries may be made into a delicious jelly or preserve that equals (some would say betters) the common cranberry jelly. And for those subject to sudden colds and sore throats: a teaspoon of rowan juice is soothing when sipped slowly or used as a gargle.

But to return full circle. Farmers may be anxious over next season's crops. Don't worry, when the berries have gone from the rowan, prune the tree and burn the prunings, then scatter the ash over the fields. That should do the trick.

As We Were

It was late one night. I had a magazine article to write and a deadline to meet. Because of this I was working long after the time that we normally went to bed.

The phone rang. It had that ominous note that all telephones have when it is late at night and a call is not expected.

"Hello: This is Andrew Fossgill, I noticed the light on and wondered if owt were wrong." I reassured him. And with a gruff apology for troubling me, he rang off.

That was the way of it in the Dales of more than forty years ago. It was the way people had of keeping an eye on each other. Had there been an emergency, a fall maybe, or a woman going suddenly and unexpectedly into labour, help would arrive as soon as possible. This "over-looking" was far removed from the insolent prying from behind lace curtains of the average suburban street. Even though the farms and cottages were scattered far and wide to either side of the dale, the sense of community was alive and well. Believe me, one felt closer to the neighbours of a mile away than other families of close proximity in urban streets or blocks of flats.

In this respect, the dale had not changed much in something like 1200 years of continuous settlement.

Even a cursory look at a map of this western part of England will show signs of those intrepid early colonists; the Vikings. Their reputation was formidable and, yes, there were the well-documented expeditions of piracy and pillage. But they gave more than they took: much more. The Norsemen preferred the solitude of autonomous farms scattered about the fellside, with some kind of central meeting point at need in the dale bottom. Each farm had its own land: tillage on the fertile alluvial soils of the floodplain, grazing around and about the main dwelling and, for summer time the saetr, the upland settlement where the livestock lived until inclement weather drove them down to winter at the main farm.

The Saxons, living in villages hacked out from the forests and set about with stockades and fences, preferred the Midlands and East Anglia.

As with so many other peoples and nations whose way of life is imperfectly understood, the Vikings were much maligned and misunderstood. The most realistic account of their entire way of life may be had from a visit to the Jorvik Museum in York. Once you know what to look for, an Ordnance Survey map will show it all, repeated over and over in the High Pennines and the Lakeland mountains and fells.

And there are many whose family names and the names of the farms themselves can be traced back to the arrival of those longboats (already established on the Isle of Man) with their human cargoes and livestock. Like those celebrated and self-willed creatures, Herdwick sheep, humans too, have an

13

invisible band that ties them to a particular spot across countless generations. This is what being a Northerner is all about.

The short history lesson can explain the idiosyncratic and indomitable nature of the true dalesman. These are the characters who figure frequently in James Herriot's books. Old habits die hard for the dalesman, not least their archaic, one might almost say Biblical, attitude to women and their rôle in society. However, if, through the evidence of their own senses, a woman should "stand proud", she became a legend.

Such a woman was a friend of ours. She was a GP in a practice that covered an enormous area of the High Pennines as well as the more pastoral reaches of Ribblesdale. Her reputation with the elderly dales farmers came not so much from her medical skills (which were considerable by any standards) but from her strength of character, her forthright manner and her ability to meet stubbornness with downright pigheadedness. All this earned her respect. What really tipped the balance in her favour was her willingness, at need, to perform urgent or even emergency veterinary duties without charging a fee. These she would do in the course of her rounds but she never went out with the intention of doing such work. That would have been unethical.

She was the same doctor who attended my wife when our son was born; at home. in a cottage almost two miles from the village. When she came to make her visits, in our area at least, she would come early; before surgery. She and my wife would often pass each other on the hill down to the village. My wife was delivering a daughter to school, with the other daughter and the baby in his cot in the back of the car.

The two drivers waved and gestured with the result that, on my wife's return home, the kettles would be on and tea would be drunk whilst the ritual inspection took place. Doctor, midwife, district nurse and emergency vet: they don't make them like that any more.

Living Proof (of what?)

There was a time, some forty years ago, that my wife trusted my map reading skills implicitly. After all, I had been a navigator in the RAF, hadn't I?

Encouraged by her arm-twisting, here are two examples of why she no longer trusts my judgement where maps are concerned.

Both of these "legitimate errors" occurred in the North Riding.

We were on holiday in Goathland. We couldn't really afford a more exotic holiday so we simply exchanged the Pennines for the North Yorkshire Moors. The holiday as a whole was a great success.

It was, of course, long before Goathland became the aorta of *Heartbeat* Country. It was, in fact, the time that *Heartbeat* actually depicts — that is the late 1950s. Goathland suited us well; a quiet, unassuming place which was willing to share its amenities with wandering sheep who grazed the grassy verges around the centre of the village.

In those days I was an enthusiastic walker. Fell-walking for me was not the pretentious business it is today. I did not indulge in expensive gear; just a Barbour jacket, waterproof trousers and plenty of pockets for food, changes of socks and the usual "boy scout" pack of compass, torch, knife and Kendal Mint cake.

My very first morning I awoke early. Wife and baby were soundly asleep so I quietly dressed, slipped out and determined to be back for breakfast.

I had a rather ineffectual map so I went up to the centre of the village where there was displayed on a weatherproof board a 2.5 inch scale map of the area. I scanned it, took note of a convenient footpath to enable me to do a circular route and cheerfully set off with a roughly drawn sketch map of the route.

Everything began superbly. I walked a road, I cut across a footpath to inspect the Roman road and continued along that same footpath whose route was etched upon my mind. Suddenly, without deviation, I found myself walking into even softer and muddier terrain. Moorland became marsh, marsh became swamp and swamp became standing water.

What was intended to be a short cut had become a nightmare. Time was getting on, my schedule was hopelessly wrong and I was going to be horribly late for breakfast. I turned round and retraced my steps.

I was late for breakfast. There were no mobile phones in those days and I had caused untold anxiety to the mind of my wife. She is not normally a worrier but there must have been something in my nature that caused her, after a late breakfast, to suggest that we both went up to the map board in the centre of the village.

And there it was; the footpath route that I had been following was clearly marked. But somehow it had metamorphosed into a contour line. I have not yet lived it down.

* * *

The other incident was even more ignominious. We were leaving Whitby and heading for Pickering. It was a route we had travelled several times before (and since). After crossing the River Esk there is a steep climb of 1:4 gradient, called Blue Bank. This above all other routes has traffic warnings, intended mainly for service buses, to engage low gear. We had never before had any problem whatsoever either going up or down. And why I should have chosen a diversion on this particular occasion I shall never know.

We were on the way up, in a suitably low gear. There must have been either a bus ahead in very low gear or a tractor. In any case there had built up a fairly long line of traffic, unwilling, or unable to pass.

Motivated only by a spirit of helpfulness I took out the map and pointed out that if we deviated at the next left turn we would cut out the traffic and make good progress by an alternative route.

Without question my wife turned off Blue Bank onto the other route. It was long, it was tortuous and in places it was 1:3.5. What is more it rejoined Blue Bank below the steepest part and, on this occasion, behind a struggling bus in low gear.

My creditability with a map sank to a rock-bottom level. Never again, in the intimacy of my family at least, has it ever risen.

Ups and Downs

Rome, history tells us, was built on seven hills. Not to be outdone, and to confirm that "Yorkshire has it all", so was Bradford. Rome's hills were impressive, as befits the one-time capital of the then accepted world. Bradford's eminences are called, with typical Yorkshire understatement, Banks. That is as in Church Bank, Horton Bank and Wibsey Bank. Even here the understatement is evidenced by the fact that Church Bank leads to Bradford Cathedral.

It is probably true to say that with one exception — the road to Bingley, Keighley and Skipton — every route out of Bradford Centre is an uphill slog.

To travel eastward out of Bradford is to enter the hinterland of Leeds. Even in a vaguely easterly or south-easterly direction, one inevitably arrives in the historically named Heavy Woollen District: Cleckheaton, Dewsbury, Batley and beyond, to Wakefield and the delights of the mining district of Castleford, Barnsley, Rotherham and Sheffield.

I can honestly say that for all its shortcomings, its "muck and brass" mentality and its narrow-mindedness in the best sense, I love this area: after all, I taught there and lectured there for many years.

But to strike out westward is to enter a different world. True, there is Halifax and Huddersfield to negotiate but by taking the high route out, up to Queensbury or Thornton and Clayton, one gets the best of all worlds. Queensbury can offer Black Dyke Mills and its celebrated brass band. There is also — if you know where to look and the weather is kind — a view of Ingleborough many miles distant.

With Thornton and Clayton, one is on the fringes of Brontë-land and all that that means to so many visitors every year. Regardless of its literary associations the view is spectacular in every direction. There is a curious mingling of bleak uplands of Nardus grass, bilberry and cotton grass, with the rise and fall of the landscape of houses and factories and mills. Now that the towns and villages are, generally, smoke-free areas, the light is good. The contrasts between the millstone grit, tarnished with weathering, and the inevitable rectangles that are cricket grounds and rugby pitches of brilliant green, is exceptional. And concerning the green of the grass we must not forget that one of the most important turf research centres is quite close at Bingley.

Curiously enough that panorama reminds me of a view-point of a very different kind. High up at the top of Sutton Bank, there is a view to inspire even the most unimaginative being.

From this edge of the Hambleton Hills there is an uninterrupted view across the plain of York. Plain is a totally inappropriate name for the exquisite beauty of one of the premier farming districts in the whole of

Britain. Here is functional beauty: landscape lovingly tended for as far as the eye can see. Well, no: not quite that far. At one extremity, with binoculars, one can see York Minster: around a great sweeping arc to the other extremity there is Darlington. It is said that on a clear day, given the time, one can follow the journey of a train from one to the other. I have never put this to the test.

The western horizon is the flank of the Pennines — irresistible to me at any time. Nearer at hand from the top of Sutton Bank, there is the jewel that is Gormire Lake. With its name, so reminiscent of Anglo-Saxon poetry, one can imagine all manner of nameless terrors hidden in its depths. On a dull day the surface is grey, like unpolished pewter — totally impenetrable and faintly menacing. When the sun shines, there is a jewel-like sparkle and a limpid clarity which reflects even the clouds and the passing birds.

In a more mundane vein, there is the gliding club and along the scarp edge the white horse carved and cared for and visible for many a mile. The whole area is one that is intrinsically beautiful in a natural way but made more so by affection and family associations. This brings me back to Wibsey Bank on the Odsal side of Bradford.

Wibsey Bank is steep, narrow and consists of uncompromising gritstone cottages that are symbolic of the textile towns of the North.

During the late fifties and early sixties we had a number of wild winters, when frost-thaw-snow produced a perilous sequence. Even during those far off years, snow did less to inconvenience the countryside than the towns. We found it straightforward travelling from Ribblesdale to Bradford to visit my in-laws. They lived near Odsal Stadium, less than a mile from Wibsey Bank. By contrast, my wife's Aunt and Uncle lived further out of town at Horton Bank Top.

The side roads were passable only on foot and the higher class roads would not give purchase to even the heaviest of vehicles. In consequence my wife's Aunt and Uncle were almost out of coal, with little immediate prospect of getting any more.

I don't know whose idea it was, but one clear and frosty night saw us together hauling a sledge laden with coal sacks up Wibsey Bank and all the way to her relations-in-distress.

To compensate — remember we were very young those forty-five or so years ago — we had a gloriously exciting ride down the snow-compacted surface of Wibsey Bank.

We arrived back at her parents' house expecting a hero's welcome. But my mother-in-law (Yorkshire to her very bones) was made of sterner stuff. We were upbraided for getting ourselves mucky and despatched to the bathroom to smarten up a bit.

I was slightly rebuffed by this reception but when I looked at myself in the mirror I could see that she had a point.

A Brush with the Brontës

Haworth on a bright July morning is not the place to be in order to discover something of the spirit of Wuthering Heights. I realised this almost as soon as I joined an escorted tour of the moor to the west of the Parsonage; being a round trip taking in the Brontë Bridge, the Brontë Falls, Top Withens and the "Brontë Lane" via Stanbury, back to the coach park, having passed through, or by, an assortment of cemeteries en route.

How I managed to become attached to a predominantly American party I shall never know. It was not an experience I wish to repeat. For the most part the tourists were of the "If it's Tuesday it must be Haworth" variety; having "done" Stratford-upon-Avon on Monday and bound, that very afternoon, for Windermere in order to "do" Dove Cottage and "Beatrix Potter Country" on Wednesday.

Amongst such cultural devotees I could do little more than tag on behind, minding my own business and trying to bring to mind the solitude and sinister nature that Emily Brontë conveys as part of her overwhelming passion for this particular piece of the gritstone Pennines. I was smitten by a tremendous desire to visit the place again; without companions and, preferably in winter.

My chance came the following December. It was not quite what I expected.

I have always had a longing to do practical, physical, things for which I am constitutionally unfitted. One of these is to walk the Pennine Way in one long, glorious trek, taking something like three weeks. The nearest I have ever come to this is to walk it piecemeal: and this I have done over a period of many years.

For some reason, an emotional urge that I cannot quite explain, I decided to walk in mid-December, the stretch from Heptonstall northwards past Top Withens and then divert from The Way and down to Oldfield, just west of Stanbury. It was something like ten miles in all. Bearing in mind that in December the best I could hope for was eight hours of daylight, I would have to push on in order to be collected by car at the other end of the route.

I set off, equipped with compass, torch and emergency rations and gear. Before I began the Way proper I diverted to Hardcastle Crags and Heptonstall village, both of which have close associations with Ted Hughes and Sylvia Plath. My companion was Mungo, the Irish setter without whose company the trip would have been quicker but much less interesting.

Most of the trek was through dull moorland made duller by the clouded sky and the wind in my face for most of the way. For half the distance Mungo ran free, never very far from me. But after a pause for lunch I felt that it would be sensible to put him on a lead; a rather long lead. This was a mixed blessing. On the one hand we were in unfamiliar country and I felt more secure attached to an animal to whom the magic words "home, boy!" would produce an almost magical and unerring response. On the other hand, it did enable me to help him along every time we passed near to where a grouse was, or had recently been sitting.

Then it began to snow. By this time we were alongside Walshaw Dean Reservoir and I checked the map, and actually used the compass in order to make for Top Withens about a mile and a half ahead. This was no gentle fluttering of flakes — the snow feathers of folk legend and lore. This was the real thing. Snow grains, the size and texture of rice grains hurtled horizontally from straight ahead. I struggled on and the setter did an excellent imitation of King Wenceslas' page, and skulked in my footsteps barely a pace behind. As quickly as it began the snow stopped. There ahead, not far away, was Top Withens. At last I knew where I was.

We struggled to the relative shelter of the ruin and I slumped down with the setter almost on top of me. The remaining third of my thermos was downed and my companion put paid to a handful of Shapes. I don't think that I even dozed off, but time just "went away" from me for long enough to make me realise that to stay where I was would be madness. In any case my face was being assaulted by an anxious tongue, which from its temperature had been savouring goodness knows what parts of his anatomy in order to get water.

The wind had changed direction and the temperature had risen enough to produce a swirling mist. Not dense fog, but enough to reflect and refract the remaining light and to give the snow a curious, icing sugar look. We set off, by compass yet again, and saw very little at all. A genuine white-out.

Then, with a swirling motion, the mist parted and there was a figure; two figures — a human and a dog. It was a huge dog. Using Mungo as a guide, it looked to be the size of a mastiff or a great dane. My first reaction was to call out for help. My second was that I had slept at Top Withens and my wife had called out the Fell Rescue. The shouts produced no result, Mungo began to snort with that curious stiffness of body that signalled his nervousness.

I have an open mind about ghosts. That is an opinion that sits well upon one by the warmth of a fireside at home. The balance of probability tips much more sharply on an open moor in winter at a site which is notoriously apt for the supernatural.

Suddenly they were gone and I bravely strode on, conscious that this was the very spot where Emily Brontë and her childhood companion, the dog Keeper, used to visit. But dogs are supposed to be psychic and Mungo barely turned his head. Sooner than I expected I saw the car. My wife thoughtfully provided really hot coffee to sustain me and also a bowl of water for Mungo who enjoyed his brisk rub down. He soon snuggled into the sleeping bag contraption that he used in the car.

Later, at home, I went over the experience again. That apparition couldn't possibly have been a ghost. It must have been a trick of the mist. But something nagged at my mind and my subconscious must have been working as I slept. At about 2.00 a.m. I awoke. I knew exactly what I had seen and what it was. I went to the bookcase and found a book about Scottish Mountaineering. I looked up Cairngorms in the index and there it was: the Grey Man of Ben McDui. It has been reliably reported that this figure has been seen on this peak under certain weather conditions. Pragmatic climbers attribute it to a projection of the climber himself onto the wall of mist. That was it! A human and a dog grotesquely misshapen: myself and Mungo. It had to be. I went back to bed and just as I was dropping off to sleep a thought occurred.

The shadow dog was big: the human small. Emily was slight and sinewy: Keeper was a mastiff.

Oh no: it couldn't have been.

The Chicken Run

When we first took our cottage in the Dales we also acquired a paddock: which was fine. However, when all the paperwork was complete, we discovered that along with the paddock we inherited a goose and a gander together with a small flock of itinerant chickens. These vagrants were unequivocally free-range. If anyone opened the gate into the paddock they would instantly appear and demand food. Once fed they would disappear without trace. It was a morning's work to comb the paddock in search of the few eggs, which were the only justification for their continuing existence. Then we discovered Tigger.

Tigger was a rough-coated terrier who lived at the next cottage on the lane. Like all terriers he was rough, tough and totally loyal to the chosen few — the choice, of course, being his.

Soon after our arrival, my wife was chatting with the elderly neighbours whilst they all waited for the weekly visit of the mobile library. The subject of hens came up and she discovered that the neighbours had a similar problem. Their problem, however, had a happier outcome. Some time around the middle of the morning they would put Tigger into their paddock with the instruction "Go fetch". He would then seek out every freely ranged egg and, with the softest of mouths, bring it to hand.

"How would you like to borrow Tigger?" we were invited. How could we refuse? The neighbours introduced us to Tigger and joined us in our paddock just to get things moving. After a couple of false starts, when he insisted on delivering only to his owners, we gradually won his confidence and every day after that he obliged after he had done the business for his owners.

It really was astounding how Tigger actually worked. Imagine simply walking on a level path with a hen's egg in your mouth. Tigger did this over and over again. He also, taking the shortest route, would jump onto a drystone wall, walk along it, jump off into the lane, back onto another wall, all without so much as cracking an egg. And he did it time after time.

It was a typically friendly Dales-type gesture. People are like that in remote rural places. The old couple were pleased to have neighbours whom they could call upon at need and we were gratified to be accepted into the community so early on.

Later, usually through the mobile library's visits, we met the others who lived in the hamlet. We were few enough in number, just three cottages and a farm down the lane and we began to participate in other matters of give and take.

The farmer used our paddock for temporary grazing and he also took a cut and baled the hay. And our geese acted as an early warning system for any intruders or suspicious characters both four legged and two.

More than any other incident these geese demonstrated the topsy-turvy way that life is lived in remote places.

The geese were vigilance personified and they sounded very aggressive. One morning I was woken up at about 5.30a.m. The geese were in full voice. It was almost like the Wildfowl Trust on a morning in February. I looked out. At first I saw nothing. Then, heading towards the far end of the paddock I saw a fox. The fox was being, literally, seen off by two vociferous and vigorously flapping geese.

It was recounting this to the neighbours that led to the solving of another mystery. Our flock of hens, after feeding and laying eggs, migrated over to their paddock where they enjoyed feeding, laying and disappearing from sight. We were sharing the same flock and didn't even suspect.

Cleaning Up

James Herriot was probably the nearest anyone ever came to being an honorary Yorkshireman. As a newly qualified vet he arrived at a practice at Thirsk between the wars. He stayed there until he died more than half a century later. He loved the place. Just look at a good, well-contoured map and you will instantly see why.

There is no need for me to paraphrase his books: they speak most eloquently for themselves. I mention him mainly because we lived, for a time, in a farm house right in the heart of his working territory. Time and again he will pop up throughout these episodes: how could it be otherwise?

I'm not quite sure how the farm house first came to our attention. At the time we were working away from North Yorkshire and we rented the place as a country retreat and holiday home. It was my hope that it might become our retirement home, if things went well. My wife, who is more practical and realistic than I am, realised at once what it took me several months to accept. It was too good to be true as a long term venture.

But even she had to admit that "it had everything". To start with it was a real farm house. The dwelling of the home farm of a small manorial estate. On two sides there were farm buildings, barns and stockyards, teeming with life. It was large, rambling and possessed of a huge kitchen which contained the first point of attraction: an Aga. Not your modern gas-fired job but a genuine old fashioned solid fuel monster which dominated one wall entirely.

The land agent who showed us round made much of this and explained how it not only provided "country farm house cooking" (I remember the phrase to this day) but also heated the water and operated the radiators throughout. Little did he realise he was wasting his breath, for he was preaching to the already converted. The downstairs rooms were spacious and lofty; the proportions elegant and aesthetically pleasing. Each of several flights of stairs led us to levels where the rooms became smaller and put increasing strain upon the vocabulary and descriptive powers of the agent. We inspected a range of outbuildings, coal sheds, wood stores and general utility rooms (all connected with the kitchen by a covered courtyard). There was a well-fenced garden and orchard which was unkempt but certainly had potential.

We were besotted and as we left, plans of various kinds were forming in our minds. Its situation, down a lane some half a mile off the A1, and entirely on its own with open country in every direction, seemed perfect. And as we drove away neither of us wondered why the tenant farmer who owned the beasts and farmed the land chose to live in a smart bungalow with "all mod cons" a little under a mile away.

We took possession in August. It took nearly until Christmas to find out.

Buying carpets and curtains was entertaining and doing it as cheaply as possible was a challenge. We embraced it by visiting places like Northallerton and Thirsk which had both warehouses and markets and catered for residents rather than tourists. Planning the garden was fun; hard work, but fun just the same. We had plans! Then the weather changed. What had been sweltering and sultry became damp and distinctly chilly. This called for the ceremonial lighting of the Aga. Wood was assembled and anthracite. Having had previous experience of an Aga of cottage rather than mansion dimensions, I set to. The outpouring of smoke and the fall of soot cannot be imagined. The connecting door to the rest of the house was hastily shut and the outside door and as many windows as would slide were opened. But not before my wife's newly applied magnolia emulsion paint had turned the colour of the walls of ancient rural inns stained by generations of tobacco smoke and untouched by human hand since the Napoleonic Wars.

We got in touch with the land agent who got onto the grapevine and produced a chimney sweep who could come "the day after tomorrow". He came at 6.45 a.m. and justified his early start by saying that there was racing at Catterick (some two miles up the road) and a horse that was owned by a syndicate he belonged to was running in the 2.30. He actually did a splendid job. He cleaned the chimney not only by getting out the soot but also by dislodging the nests (and corpses)

33

of several jackdaws. He cleaned up very well and said we were not to light any fires in the open grates until he had seen to them, and that wouldn't be until a week on Tuesday. He also cleaned up in another sense because the horse he was part owner of came in at 33/1.

The constraint upon open fires was not too great in rooms where there were radiators connected to the Aga. Elsewhere we had to rely upon Calor gas and an excessive use of electric heaters. This did troublesome things to the fuse box and necessitated another call to the land agent who, through the grapevine or the old boy network unearthed a diagnostic electrician who could come "a week on Thursday". Was this alright? I hastily checked with the clerk of the course at Catterick Racecourse and agreed terms. In a word the diagnosis was rewiring: the entire house. Christmas was fast approaching and our son and his wife were coming for the holiday.

We all have a sense of humour, fortunately, and soon got used to uprooted floorboards and stray lengths of flex that appeared and disappeared in alarming places. But Christmas was fun. We made good use of the few truly habitable rooms; and with an Aga, who could really complain if much of the time was spent in the kitchen, which soon took on the appearance of E. H. Shepard's evocative illustrations of Badger's kitchen in *The Wind in the Willows*. And what better model could we have?

In spite of the inconveniences and the irritations we had, we did have a gloriously happy time there. But as a permanent proposition it was not to be. As we drove away for the last time onto the A1 and south there was sadness mingled with a sense of relief. For months afterwards we had sent to us through the post the *Northern Echo* and the *Stockton* and *Darlington Gazette*.

Mainly to see if that tenant farmer's bungalow with "all mod cons" ever came onto the market.

Country Sports

Most country sports are part of rural life and go far deeper into society than many people realise who either condemn them for political reasons or who indulge in disruptive and useless activities. I put into this category the "kidnapping" of beagle packs and the releasing into the wild of mink. This latter act can only result in the destruction of the countryside as we know it and love it.

I enjoy country sports. I have taken part in many although I have never ridden to hounds. This is because I have never met anyone stupid enough to lend me a horse to ride cross-country! It wouldn't be fair to the horse, although the sight of it might amuse (or stimulate the contempt of) any fox preparing to give hounds a run for their money.

Yes, there are people who genuinely have moral doubts about hunting. Them I respect. Those who, by contrast, wilfully abuse the genuine feelings of those same objectors and use them for their own political or anarchistic ends, I despise.

Enough preaching! What follow are anecdotes of specific instances when some aspect or another gave me that warm glow of contentment; or made me yet again marvel at the joyousness of being a countryman surrounded by country folk.

Having been a schoolteacher and lecturer I tend to know better than anyone else! That's the theory anyway. In real life things are somewhat different and I often end up with figurative egg on my face. It happened once at a team chase held high up in the South Pennines near to Emley Moor mast.

We lived in a farm cottage attached to a livery stable. The farmer and his family hunted with the local hunt and it was at their daughter's farm that the team chase annually took place. The actual course-building was done with skill and great integrity, the terrain was good and varied. There were several natural obstacles, such as fallen trees and ditches mixed in with the built fences and walls. It was generally agreed that the course was one of the best in the whole of the North of England.

On the day of the chase my wife and I invariably joined in as fence judges. A fence judge is exactly what its name suggests; to see fair play and to judge whether the competitor jumped "between the flags". One or more of the fences were what are called dressing fences. This is where all four riders of a team (or at least two of them) jump exactly together. Apart from this it is every team member for him (or her) self. And the first three home count in the placings.

We did this job for several years and we always took with us Mungo, the setter, who usually curled up during the actual rounds and kept clear of the flailing feet when the fence was actually in use. His presence was not absolutely necessary but he was a country dog and loved all things equestrian; from tormenting the notorious Sorcery in her own paddock to being almost decapitated at Wetherby Races by being too eager on the rails.

Naturally the memories flood back whenever I think about those years. Most of them are memories of warmth and joy at simply being a part of such an event. One memory, however, stands out for a somewhat different reason. It was my first year on duty and I was immensely pleased with myself, especially when, inspecting my fence, some of the riders from other hunts walked the course to iron out possible problems and also to decide upon a line of approach that would give them the edge.

The party who approached my fence on this particular occasion was the Durham Farmers. They were strung out, each inspecting their own potential problem points. The leader approached my fence and we passed the time of day. He was friendly and asked a question or two which prompted me to expound at length about the best way to jump the fence, how to approach it and where to take off for maximum forward momentum. The rider listened politely and slipped in the odd question or two. Then a voice.

"Hello, I see you know Brian already. I'm Mark and these are . . ." I forget whom. My blank look at being expected to know a visitor whom I had never met before prompted the additional remark "Brian Fletcher".

It was a very chilly day and I was well wrapped up. Even so a warm glow started in my stomach and crept remorselessly up my neck and face. I had failed to recognise the man to whom I was giving naïve and probably useless information. Two years earlier and the year before that, Brian Fletcher had won the Grand National on Red Rum!

With all agriculture at a low ebb, and hill farming particularly distressed, farmers are having to diversify or go under. Some do bed and breakfast and convert barns into holiday cottages. Others, in lowland regions, build golf ranges or go into fish farming by excavating pits or flooding quarries.

One farmer, whom I know, supplemented his income in a most ingenious way. For one day a week he opened his farm to visitors who came to watch the sheepdog displays. These were not trials: they were dogs practising their skills over real country and not over a constructed course. There was no competition. It was simply the routines of the day performed before an audience.

I think he charged £5 per car for parking.

Before the display proper the farmer explained the rudiments of shepherding, dog training and dog working. He also explained the techniques of using the whistle. It was everything that an interested visitor needed to know to appreciate the one branch of farming that is still done in the time honoured way: just a man, a couple of dogs and the sheep. And remember, for all the advances in nutrition and animal welfare over the past fifty years or so, sheep are still, fundamentally, wild creatures. One gets the feeling that what happens before the watching crowds has been going on similarly since Old Testament times.

The display involved a single dog work and brace work. Nothing fanciful like driving sheep up ladders or "circus tricks" like that. Just simple lifting, fetching, penning and handling sheep. It was done with one dog and two and the distinctive signals for each dog prevented confusion.

As a finale the same drill was performed again using a flock of geese instead of sheep. This, I'm told, is a favourite trick of dog handlers who train dogs with limited resources and perhaps a paddock or small field instead of a farm. The principle is exactly the same since, apparently, sheep and geese respond in very similar ways. One thing is for certain: both activities produced an enthusiastic response from the spectators.

It also drew another response when we were there. Tied to the back bumper of the Land Rover was a collie puppy of about seven months or so. He was right at the start of his training and a joy to see. With every signal to either of the working dogs, to every movement of the flock, to every successful activity, he responded with such enthusiasm. He simply couldn't keep still. He danced about to the limit of his restraint. When the signal "down!" was given he sat and shuffled his bottom in the dust. Believe me, no human pupil could ever show such enthusiasm for a task that was to occupy his waking hours for the rest of his active life.

Country Fare

The tea room had everything necessary to manifest the true nature of a market town: several rooms up rickety stairs, widely separated tables, chintzy easy chairs with low tables, just for taking morning coffee. Every surface was covered with gingham and, mercifully, no muzak intruded upon the local chat. In imitation of more illustrious places elsewhere, there was a plentiful supply of newspapers; local newspapers. I counted the *Craven Herald*, the *Westmorland Gazette*, the *Northern Echo* and a stray copy of the *Telegraph* and *Argus* (left, no doubt, by a visitor from Morecambe).

It was definitely a place for residents and not tourists. This was confirmed by two facts. It flourished out of season even more than from Easter to October, and on market days (Tuesday and Saturday for the street market and Saturday only for the livestock) two rooms were set aside for serving full meals to country folk and stall holders.

It was the kind of place where everyone trusted everyone else. Bags of shopping did not have to be humped upstairs to the table. They could be left in a little room behind the paydesk and collected on leaving.

Opposite the paydesk there was an ordering place, behind that was a kitchen and that was all there was to the ground floor, except for the dumb waiter next to the stairs. It fascinated me to see that when an order was made up and despatched upwards in the dumb waiter a bell was rung and waitresses on the appropriate floor would serve to the table.

It was, without exception, all good country fare. It was no more "country fayre" than it was an "Olde Tea Shoppe". Much of the food was organic. This was presented without broadcasting the fact either by name or excessive price. The carrot cake was especially good and so was the parkin and the apple pie. Without question, the pie was served with a generous slice of Wensleydale cheese. Such is the custom in the north and the cheese was also offered with rich fruit cake.

This wealth of detail is intended to stress the traditional, one has to say old-fashioned, aspects of the place. There were other cafes, of course, and snack bars and no Yorkshire town would be complete without a chippy or two. Some of the pubs served food but there was nowhere else quite like Pam's Pantry. It is the kind of place, which, when it does finally give up, will be conveyed intact to somewhere like Beamish Museum, which is dedicated to preserving the traditional way of life.

I knew that cafe years ago. Even now it remains in the safe hands of the same family, although the staff changes every so often. Girls leave to "better themselves" as they did twenty years or so ago. In modern terms they will move on to try their luck in the more congenial atmosphere of Bradford or Leeds or even Middlesborough or Stockton.

It was just such an aspiring townee who gave me a quiet laugh recently. After a long absence from the area, my wife and I returned for a holiday and went along to Pam's Pantry for old times' sake. Nothing seemed to have changed. The toasted tea cakes were still superb, the parkin was moist and tangy. The teapot was generously full and the teabags (progress indeed here!) plentiful. The menu even went to the trouble of informing us that it was Yorkshire Tea. nothing seemed to have changed yet there was a feeling of progress in the air. It was indefinable.

The clue to the "winds of change" blew over us as we left. The staircase was still narrow and as we descended one of the young waitresses was coming up. As my wife and I moved into single file, the girl moved to the side and gave us an unexpectedly broad smile.

It was clearly a smile of anticipation. She was carrying a large brown paper bag. It was visibly filled and the smell of it was encouraging. It was clearly labelled McDonalds. Could it have been?

Crossroads

Arching high above the Scammonden Valley, running, apparently, to infinity both to the east and to the west, is the M62. As a road it is a success story, a feat of civil engineering, but not, as some have described it a groundbreaking link between east and west Pennine communication.

Unlike previous trans-Pennine roads, the M62 pays little regard to the relief or surface quality of the countryside. It has little concern either for settlement or communication en route. Older roads — that can be traced back to the greenways and pack-horse routes — were there to serve existing settlements. Or, to look at it in a mirror, so to speak, settlements grew up (around an inn perhaps) to serve the needs of the drovers and their herds. Entire books can be (indeed they have been) written about drovers and greenways. Some are romantic and highly charged emotional tales: others are severely prosaic and academic. To anyone who loves the Pennines — especially the gritstone Pennines to the south of the Aire gap — as I do, they are enchantment.

Enchantment means being under a spell. In this instance the most potent place of all is the aptly named, forbidding spot called Blackstone Edge.

Blackstone is one of a number of "edges" or outcrops of millstone grit: Stanage and Froggatt are two more. Edges run like exposed black vertebrae along the spine of the Pennines. At any time of day, indeed, in any kind of weather, Blackstone is the quintessential Pennine landscape. One thinks of the poetry of Ted Hughes; one expects characters from the Brontë novels and poems to come into view. One agrees with the seventeenth century traveller, Celia Fiennes, that Blackstone Edge was "noted all over England for a dismal high precipice". And she had her own view about the almost supernatural miasma that infected the place . . . "these high hills stagnate the air and hold the mist and rains almost perpetually."

She must have caught it on a bad day, after an indigestible meal the night before. When the sun shines, casting shadows before you, the view into Lancashire is, literally, breathtaking. One gasps with amazement or delight. There are shades of green and blue that shimmer and blend with distance. The trite expression "roof of the world" comes to life.

But it is not the distance that really takes hold of the imagination. That is underfoot. It is called the Roman road, but some authorities doubt its provenance. Whatever its origin, it is a paved track across Blackstone Edge — some 1500 feet above sea level. At 18 feet wide (twice the average packhorse road) the trackway has a shallow channel running down the middle, like a drain.

Curiously enough it occurs only on the Lancashire side of the Edge. To the east it joins with a natural rock platform called Dhoul's Pavement.

45

The question to ask is: why Blackstone Edge? There are easier crossing points, gentler gradients on both the Yorkshire and the Lancashire sides. Why, at this particular spot, should there be at least four routes? The most up-to-date is the modern A58. This is modified from an old turnpike (toll) road dating back to about 1800. There are signs of an even older turnpike. These were both toll roads and the traffic using them must have been enough to pay for their upkeep. It does not take much imagination to feel the hustle and bustle of a pre-industrial age blending into the first outflowing of the Industrial Revolution: of wool and cotton; of trade and industry; of skies blackened on either flank by the smoke of mill chimneys. Even the coal was local.

In addition to these "official" roads there was also an ancient packhorse way. This is perhaps the most romantic of all: cloth collected from outlying farms that were also isolated mills; salt from Cheshire to preserve food and to help to dye the cloth: and luxury, even exotic goods brought in from foreign lands when the trade ships flourished.

All these thoughts (and more) passed through my mind and my senses were totally in the past. I was suddenly brought back to the present by a voice asking; "how much further down is Ripponden?" Three youth hostellers had climbed up by the Old Road from Littleborough. They were young and enthusiastic and kitted out with all the latest gear. As they waved a parting they were transformed in my eyes first into

46

mediaeval merchants, and then, as distance distorted my vision, they became monks on a pilgrimage.

So vivid were these images that I wondered why they had spoken to me in the vernacular of Lancashire and not in the more measured tones of Middle English.

I was alone once more. The distance had become blurred and indistinct, a breeze became a blow and I headed for the A58 and the car. The best of the day had come and gone and the wind had a bite that drove me on at speed. There was a traffic jam on the A58 caused by people returning from a day out at Hollingworth Lake. At some point along the road we crossed the Pennine Way. And as I always do whenever I cross it or trek a part of it, I promised myself that one day, one day as yet unspecified, I would take it on from Edale to Kirk Yetholm.

A promise not fulfilled: so far. But one day — I might even get a book out of it. And then again . . .

Getting the Bird

Our resident magpies operate on our behalf what must be the most efficient early warning system in the whole of the natural world. No visitor, two legged or four, can come anywhere near the garden without the most unholy chattering accompanied by much sweeping and hovering. Sometimes this is simply a nuisance; other times I have had glimpses of birds and animals I might otherwise have missed. That was the case one morning.

The magpies started even earlier than usual at about 6.45a.m. They chattered and yelled abuse; they flapped frantically about from tree to fence and back again. But they avoided a sycamore altogether until bravado took one of them in a high spiralling swing about it. The others, not to be outdone in bravery, followed.

Then I saw the target of their antics.

She sat half hidden by foliage, her long slaty-grey tail balancing her on the bough. A sparrowhawk, so I thought. Then she flew off, and I knew at once that this was no sparrowhawk, though I might be excused for thinking so. It was a full grown female cuckoo.

The cuckoo is probably the only bird that literally everyone can recognise by voice alone and which very few can recognise on sight. Years ago, before migration was understood, people used to think that in winter the cuckoo changed into the sparrowhawk.

They are superficially similar — hence my mistake. Other legends and rumours abound but my favourite is the Yorkshire folk tale about the residents of Austwick in the Dales, where I used to live. The story goes like this.

Being simple folk the natives noticed that when the cuckoo flew off, winter was on the way. To hang on to the summer they decided to prevent the cuckoo's flight and to this end they built a high wall about the place. Their strenuous efforts not only exhausted their bodies but tired their wits as well so that they forgot to make a roof over the place. Naturally the bird flew off over the top of the wall. Residents of nearby Horton-in-Ribblesdale heard about it and nicknamed the natives Austwick Cuckoos; a name that they bear to this day.

I watched my cuckoo swing up and soar over the garden wall, seen off at a discreet distance by the magpies. As she escaped from the confines of the garden she called once. It was a call of mingled triumph and contempt for her pursuers. In some sense, too, a commentary upon those far off Austwick ancestors.

Curses and Curses

Have you ever noticed how easy it is, when out in the country, to strike up a conversation with total strangers? On this occasion it was brought about by the title of a magazine a fellow walker had tucked into the outside pocket of her day-sack. It was the Journal of Alternative & Complementary Medicine.

As we talked, complementary medicine led to folk medicine and, inevitably, to folklore. Then, as all true ramblers have a habit of doing, we stopped somewhere out in the country and simply considered the landscape in companionable silence. There were fields and hedgerows and patches of woodland. Dog roses and hawthorns glowed red with hips and haws; bramble bushes swarmed over a boundary hedge laden, with blackberries — almost pickable without stirring from the stile that we leant on. And in the corner of the field, alone but for some rank grasses around its feet, an elder tree grew. Its branches were quite weighed down with gleaming black fruit.

There, ready to hand, was a conversational gambit guaranteed to last the rest of the walk back to the central car park.

Why, according to folklore and folk medicine, does the elder have such an ambiguous reputation? On the one hand it provides flowers and fruit to make delicious wines and cordials: on the other it is regarded as an evil tree — deemed to be unlucky to all who meddle with its wood.

My fellow traveller brought dignity and expertise to the conversation. I contributed childhood memories of sixty years ago concerning the ways of village "wise women" of the kind who flourished, in out-of-the-way villages, right up to the Second World War.

The elder goes back in folk medicine to the ancient Egyptians. Its use was cosmetic (Elderflower water being used as a skin cleaner and astringent). It is also a soothing lotion in cases of sunburn. Taken internally the elderflower decoction was mixed with peppermint extract and used to alleviate coughs and colds. These uses, along with the making of preserves and jellies from the berries, ought to have made the growing of elder trees almost obligatory in every cottage garden in the land.

But for every benefit this unusual tree bestows, there is a corresponding prohibition. I knew many of these from childhood. The wood must not be burned in a fireplace; must never be used for making furniture — or boats; and especially not to be used in making babies' cradles.

Old wives' tales perhaps but my knowledgeable companion took me back in mind to pagan times. To the time before ancient Greece and Rome we travelled; to when the moon goddess of the ancient world had the elder as her sacred tree. A tentative shiver ran through me as I heard of the misfortunes that would befall any who had the temerity to cut down an elder tree without first chanting an incantation to the "earth mother" who dwelt inside.

"Old girl, give me of thy wood and I will give you some of mine when I grow into a tree."

Then the tree could be chopped down. But what use is it if it cannot be burned or built with? Curiously enough branches of the elder when gathered on May Day were supposed to be used to cure the bite of a rabid dog. "But how?" I asked. My companion did not know. She did, however, offer me a thoroughly practical use for the wood. Back in the days when hearses were drawn by a matched pair of horses decorated with black plumes and harness, the handle of the driver's whip had to be made from elder wood. This was to protect him from the influences of the spirits of the recently dead; especially those whose deaths were violent or tragic.

Compared with this my contribution was mundane but very practical. Nothing will flourish under the shade of an elder tree, to the perimeter extent of the root system at least. That being so, the sensible gardener will site his compost heap in the shade of an elder tree. The tree secretes a substance which hastens the natural fermentation of the compost. This compost will, in turn, enrich the tree, bringing, one can but hope, favourable responses for the composting gardener from the Queen of the Night herself.

Who knows?

Random Customs

Sporting purists distinguish between Lawn Tennis and Real Tennis and devotees of the latter regard Lawn Tennis as a commercial undertaking and nothing more.

The game of Rugby also has its own dichotomy. Rugby Union and Rugby League. Union is the posh version, the game that began — so we are led to believe — at Rugby school when a certain Webb-Ellis picked up the ball in a game of soccer, ran the length of the pitch and scored the very first try. The story is well-known and acknowledged in Rugby by statues and museums. Which has to make Rugby School the first Webb-site in the world!

Until recently Union was the amateur game, played by ex-public school boys and University men and supported by a certain breed of Welsh men whose combination of gymnastics, ballet and sheer guts brought them to the very forefront of the national and international game.

Participants tend to be scornful of Rugby League which, from its very outset was a professional game played throughout the north and regarded by spectators and participants alike as a continuation of the Wars of the Roses (which elsewhere in the UK ended with the Battle of Bosworth).

For all its gritty, plebeian associations "League" has its folklore too; and a very romantic beginning it was: almost a "once upon a time" story. At Haxey, near Doncaster, many centuries ago Lady Mowbray was riding to church to celebrate "old" Christmas Day (the 6th January). A strong wind blew off her hood and tossed it away. Twelve labourers dashed after it to rescue it. The Lady was so pleased with the courtesy and mannerly behaviour of the labourers that she gave to the village a piece of land, known since then as "The Hoodlands". Moreover, she provided annually a hood to be thrown and fought over at the place where her original hood was captured. This activity developed into an annual game which was subsequently formalised into the game of Rugby (League, of course.)

Another custom — which has never been seen by me but vouched for by several others — was a horse race inaugurated in the reign of Richard III by the Earl of Burlington and modified in 1664.

It is a race that is run over four miles, approximately the same distance as the Grand National. The race is run cross country over a course of Roman roads and country lanes near Market Weighton on the third Thursday in March. It is regarded as the most strenuous horse race in England.

It is never advertised and, allegedly, has been run in an unbroken sequence since 1664. To add to the mystery, no-one knows until 11.00 a.m. on the actual day whether there will be a race or not.

* * *

Another custom of extreme antiquity, which again is hearsay, is the so-called Penny Hedge or Horngarth planting on the Eve of Ascension Day. In 1159 at Whitby, North Yorkshire, three local landowners allegedly murdered a priest, in the forest where they were hunting, because he gave refuge to a kid and a wild boar they had wounded.

The penalty involves planting a hedge of wood, cut from the same forest, on Whitby sands. The hedge has to withstand three tides without being washed away. At the conclusion three blasts are sounded on a horn reputed to be 800 years old.

I make no excuse for using words such as "allegedly" and "so-called" because in their very nature these tales are highly local and passed down by word of mouth from one generation to another. Since such fireside tale-telling is now a dead art, thanks to video games and computers, I feel that it is a good thing to preserve some of these customs, no matter how incomplete and corrupted they may now be.

Being a Dalesman

Despite learning quite early the futility of ever being accorded the distinction of "Yorkshire Folk", I set about becoming A Dalesman. This is a title that may be earned, and it is a treasured acceptance indeed. However, there is a snag. This is how I found out about it, snag and all.

I was talking one day with a friend who is both a Dalesman and a "proper Yorkshireman". He listened with sympathy to my tale of woe with mutterings and much shaking of the head. "Aye," He seemed to commune with the collie that lay at his feet. " First things first." With the same gentleness that he used when taking a sheepdog puppy through its early stages of training, he questioned me.

Was I born in the Dales? No, I wasn't. But my father used to live and work near Pateley Bridge when he was a lad and used to walk to Harrogate to watch Holmes and Sutcliffe open for Yorkshire. This was an impressive claim but it was dismissed with a regretful shake of the head.

And so it was that I learned the hard way. Just as there are levels of esteem in the national honours like M.B.E., O.B.E., C.B.E., and so on, so there are levels of qualification for the title Dalesman.

The basic (or obvious) one is qualification by birth. Simple you might think, but not so. There is a strict limiting factor as to what a "dale" actually is. Every Yorkshire child used to be taught the mnemonic SUNWAC. This is an acronym for the Yorkshire Dales from north to south: Swale, Ure, Nidd, Wharfe, Aire and Calder. Residents of the first three qualify for the full length of the river — right up to its confluence with the Yorkshire Ouse. The residents of the upper reaches of the Wharfe and Aire, which include some of the bleakest scenery in the entire Pennines, are definitely dalesmen by birth. Regrettably these rivers, along with the Calder and Colne, run down into the industrial excesses of Leeds, Bradford, Huddersfield, Halifax, Wakefield and Dewsbury. Residents here are definitely not dalesmen by birth. But they may well be "Yorkshire Folk" regardless. Confusing, isn't it?

To make things even more confusing, a dalesman by birth may well be outside this close-knit and cosy SUNWAC confederation. To the north of the Swale there are Teesdale, Weardale and the dales of the South & North Tyne. To the west of the Pennine watershed there are Ribblesdale, Lunesdale and the Eden Valley.

More clear-cut is the Three Peaks qualification. When I first took an interest in the Dales, this was a legitimate measure of "dalesmanship". One had to complete within twelve hours the round trip of visiting the summit of Ingleborough, Whernside and Penyghent. It used to be a very challenging test of stamina and determination. Nowadays, with special diets, power training and personal trainers, the trip has lost a great deal of its exclusiveness. It may even be downgraded and lose its status altogether.

My friend then told me that by far the least known qualifier was the invention of Fred Heardman of Edale. During his heyday between the wars this most intrepid of all Pennine walkers devised several walks and routes. Pre-eminent amongst them, and having a serious claim to conferring dalesman status, is the "Four Inns" walk. Nowadays, in fact, there are only three inns. The evocatively named Isle of Skye Inn, above Holmfirth, is now defunct. The others are the Snake Inn, the Nag's Head at Edale and the Cat and Fiddle high up on the Buxton to Macclesfield road in the Derbyshire Peak District.

Painfully and painstakingly I began training for the Three Peaks race. Sadly the training never got beyond the planning stage and I gave up in the end. The more I thought about it, the more convinced I became that this qualification for dalesmanship was seriously flawed. Here I was, resident in one of the most dramatic and picturesque parts of the entire Pennine chain. Not only that, I was gainfully employed in a way that benefitted the community as a whole. All this and I was still denied the coveted title of Dalesman.

What really turned the blade in the heart was the fact that, in summer time at least, coach parties came out from Bradford or Leeds — or even from Manchester, Bolton, Bury and Wigan — in order to enable youths from those towns to qualify as dalesmen without having any residential qualifications whatsoever. The coaches crammed the car park at Horton-in-

Ribblesdale; the travellers "signed in" or registered in the Three Peaks book in the Cafe and that was it. They walked, they returned in less than twelve hours, signed out and away. By the time most of them got back, the pubs had shut so they didn't even put cash into the local economy.

All those years I was a frustrated Dalesman. Eventually, after we had moved further south to the bleak uplands where the rivers Colne and Calder rose, I qualified almost accidentally.

For the first time I had the opportunity to have and run a small flock of sheep: well, five actually. They were my pride and joy and I ran them on a small piece of land with a miniature lambing pen. For breeding purposes these ewes were literally farmed out to a local farmer who ran them with his own flock of some 250.

For reasons which I no longer remember they had to be registered. I was thus, without even trying, their registered shepherd or flockmaster. And that was it. By so doing I became a Dalesman automatically.

My wife tells me I have a perverse side to my nature. Although I do not agree with her I have to admit that this "backdoor entry" into the Dalesman Fold gave me a perverse satisfaction: for two reasons. I was now no longer a real Dalesman in the territorial sense. I qualified because I was a flockmaster. But the sheep that qualified me were not Yorkshire sheep at all. They were Derbyshire Gritstone crossed with a Suffolk tup!

The Village that Died

This particular village died. It was not drowned beneath the waters of a reservoir: a fate which ensured at least a body of legend. A romance that would compensate for the one-time clangour of church bells and the buzz, hum and chatter of the school playground.

No! This village died from neglect: by being cut off from the main stream of life. And it had nobody to blame but itself. To save its blushes I shall call it Laxdale.

For centuries Laxdale had been the nucleus of a farming community scattered about the fellside in companionable isolation. In the days I remember it was almost self-sufficient, as far as everyday needs were concerned. Everything else was available on market days from the nearby town. There was even a village hall that turned itself into a doctor's surgery once a week.

The farms were occupied by old-established families: Mason, Metcalfe and Keartons. Inter-married and inbred, they collectively owned some 14,000 sheep: Dalesbred and Swaledales for the most part. And farmers and villagers alike — as a side line only — did well with bed and breakfast.

In fact, the only "down side" was that the village was bisected by a main road, which was a tourist route to the Lakes. Of the two determining factors in the demise of Laxdale this was by far the more important. The other was a chain reaction which began with the death of Charlie Mason.

Charlie was the one member of the Mason clan who didn't farm. Charlie was a blacksmith and farrier. Like all the Masons he did well. His frugality was legendary and his diet was as limited as his powers of conversation. He had become increasingly taciturn since the death of his wife — some ten years earlier — and he had never quite recovered. It was rumoured by many in the village that when he set the table for meals, he still set places for two!

Be that as it may, it was because of Miriam — or of her family to be more precise — that the decline of the village came about. Miriam Clifford's family were a minor branch of a textile dynasty from Keighley. How they met and why she consented to marry Charlie Mason was still being debated right up to her death.

Charlie was devastated: not simply because he had been deprived of the partner of what had been a love match, but because his grand scheme had come crashing down. Ever a rebel, a younger son without a farm to inherit, he struck out on his own. This was unconventional. He married an off-comed 'un which was unusual. But the rumour that he was planning to remove to Malton and set up as a farrier, plating racehorses; that was downright unreasonable.

It all came to nothing. And then Charlie himself died and that did it! Soon after Miriam had died, Charlie changed his will. The Masons up at Cross Gill got

61

nothing; neither did the Metcalfes. But the Keartons at Beckside; they got the smithy with the stock. This was in token of the fact that Jack Kearton's father had lent Charlie the money to set up the smithy in the first place — a debt that had been paid off years ago.

What came as a shock was the disposition of the residue of the estate. That went to Miriam's younger brother Richard. The legacy was mainly the freehold on three cottages in the village and the four acre field that was leased to the school as a playing field and school garden, a substantial income in itself.

There was talk of new brooms sweeping clean. Richard increased the cottage rents to the very limit of fairness (and many said beyond). Two tenants wound up their local affairs and left, the third was soon to follow.

As an investment Richard Clifford refurbished the cottages and advertised them for holiday lettings.

Then coincidence moved in and took a hand. For years there had been murmurings and rumblings from the Parish Council and representations to the County. The need for a by-pass to take a danger burden away from the village and speed the through traffic on its way.

High level talks, involving landowners, councillors, civil engineers and contractors went along smoothly. A by-pass was accepted in principle and implemented in fact with remarkable speed and efficiency.

Changes took place. The school was deemed no longer cost effective and closed down. The lease on the playing field and garden reverted to Richard Clifford.

The third of old Charlie's cottages which had been rented by the school teacher, was handed back to Richard Clifford. School Meadow was converted to an exclusive development of "executive style" properties.

That was it really. The village lost its shop, its pub had a make-over and emerged as something "Ye Olde", part of a large brewery chain. The village hall was disposed of and the doctor became part of a large health centre in town. Saddest of all for some, the travelling library no longer appeared every Thursday at the edge of the green. It did, however, continue to stop at an outlying hamlet further up the Dale. There it was regularly used by the Masons, the Metcalfes and the Keartons from their outlying farms.

Thus it was that the village effectively, died, as a village that is. It became a detached suburb. After all, how many villages do you know where the houses that cluster round the village green are inhabited by two solicitors, an accountant and two estate agents?

The Kearton's of Beckside had the last word. They sought planning permission to establish a camping and caravanning site with on-site activities and entertainments. The humour of the situation lay in the fact that High Road — the other way out of the side dale — had a gradient of 1:4.

Every van that visited Beckside, every camper van and tent, had therefore to drive from the by-pass and through the village to get to its pitch.

Requiescat (but not In Pacem).

Animals in Disguise

High up on the roof of the Pennines, between Edale and Marsden, you will sometimes see, if you go high enough and far enough into the wilds, the mountain hare. This is the variety, common in the Scottish Highlands, that changes from its dark summer colour to a winter white.

Where I live, some 250 feet lower than the tops, the "normal" hare is the common lowland type which is brown or sandy coloured all the year round. Very rarely a vagrant that is white, or partly so, will come down low enough to be sighted on the moors above our village. It happened last weekend.

All week I had been kept in by a combination of bad weather and a heavy cold. I hadn't wanted to go out but my dog — an Irish setter who usually gets something like ten miles free running every day — had become restless with the accumulated restraint of several days lead walking round the roads. So I took to the hills to blow away the last vestiges of a throbbing head and stuffy nose. It did the trick.

Mungo, true to his training and breeding, put up a number of hares that he had patiently quested and found but he has been trained not to chase either "fur or feather" and I watched them into the distance and out of sight. Actually out of sight was only a few yards because these were the common hare whose colours blended well with the background. Then, towards dusk, he put up a partly white mountain hare that ran well and was visible, owing to its colour, far away over the fell side. Had there been snow on the ground it would have been invisible almost from the outset.

This incident made me wonder about the mountain hare in particular and animal camouflage in general. Why do mountain hares change colour in the winter time? How do they do it? What triggers off the change to white and also the change back again for the summer?

Quite clearly they change to resemble their background; a form of protective colouring. To say with certainty why they do it is less easy. It is facile and wrong to say that the hares know that winter is on the way and change accordingly. Yet I once heard a college student on teaching practice say just that, along with several more equally anthropomorphic statements.

With some species it is a rise or fall in temperature that causes the change. But this cannot be the cause of the hare's change can it? Otherwise this unusually mild winter would have prevented any alteration in the colour of the coat. No. It is a variation in the duration of daylight hours and changes in the intensity of the sunlight that does it.

As the days grow shorter after the Autumn equinox, and the strength of the sun lessens, the ability of the hare to manufacture pigments to colour the fur declines. Thus the fur turns white. This explains why the colour of truly Arctic species of many animals is white for most of the time.

This theory was put to the test some years ago by Russian scientists who took a large number of Arctic hares in full winter coat and divided them into groups. One group was exposed to varying amounts of artificial light; a second group was kept in the dark; and a third group was given a more than normal radiation of light. The results were interesting. Group one was summer coated by March; Group two was still quite white in June; and Group three had become summer coated as early as January.

We are only just beginning to realise the potent effect of light upon the life cycles of animals. For example, it is the day-length and intensity of light that stimulates the sexual cycle in sheep. This is why lambing time in the south of England is many weeks earlier than in Scotland or here in my native Pennines.

To return to camouflage of a different kind: this characteristic of both the animal and plant kingdoms makes a very satisfactory project for pupils of almost any age. It need not be restricted to mammals; in fact, it is not possible to do so in the classroom; but can embrace all the orders of living things — especially insects.

You can start with stick insects. There are several kinds and they can be kept very easily in the classroom or lab. From there you can go on to other imitative species, including those mimics like the Syrphids; a family of flies that survive by mimicking the appearance and habits of the fierce wasps, bees and hornets.

Again and again, by protective colouring, by special resemblance, by colour changes like those of the chameleon as well as by colour disguises, like the hare we began with, you will find an unsuspected world of complexity and confusion awaiting discovery and study. Not least of the advantages of this kind of biology is the complete freedom from expensive apparatus and detailed, specialist, knowledge.

In time you may even become a specialist yourself because there is still plenty to find out.

I may even have found out something new myself — I have never seen any reference to this phenomenon anywhere. Once again, it involves Mungo.

We were up on the hills and he was questing keenly in a bank of bracken and willowherb. The colour of bracken and setter are almost the same and I could barely see him. I walked into the bracken and called. then I noticed, for the first time, that the smell of wet bracken crushed underfoot is almost identical with the smell of wet dog. Could this be another natural disguise to help a predator to get right up to its keen scented prey? Or am I being fanciful?

That Loveliest Walk

Back in the 1920s a group of writers on country matters met to discuss "Britain's Most Lovely Walk." The group included John Masefield and Hilaire Belloc. Beyond that I know nothing at all. No minutes; no transcript of speeches; no latter-day Boswells to immortalise latter-day Johnsons. Nothing that I can dredge up. One can simply speculate.

It is, however, most likely that every one of the walks discussed and even agreed about was in the Downs, the Cotswolds or the Chilterns. Those were the haunts of the aesthetic, Neo-Georgians. They were also the home of such true country lovers as Kenneth Grahame.

Step back a century and a very different location emerges. We are in the landscapes of the North: the Malham of Charles Kingsley; the Haworth of the Brontës; the Lakes of Wordsworth et al. Just to imagine those locations is to summon up any number of lovely walks. But not one of the writers would presume to designate a "Loveliest Walk": just a favourite one or two.

The Wordsworths (as we have shown elsewhere) were prodigious walkers. It was a perfectly natural thing to do; for utilitarian reasons, not just aesthetic gratification.

* * *

I cannot think of a more delightful excursion than to accompany Dorothy Wordsworth on one of her favourite walks. It is not perversity, either, to want to do so in William's absence. William spent a great deal of time away from Grasmere during the early years of the 19th century. Much of it in East Yorkshire making plans for his marriage to Mary Hutchinson.

When he was away, devoted Dorothy kept a diary that meticulously chronicled every detail of her day "that I might give William pleasure by it".

It is almost certain that Dorothy's "loveliest walk" was the four miles or so that began and ended at Dove Cottage and circumnavigated Rydal Water, going near to Rydal Mount — which was the last and most imposing of their Lakeland homes. The walk is one that avoids roads for the most part and doing it today, even with the tourist traffic hurtling by on the B5287, one gets something of the tranquility and solemnity that Dorothy felt on her solitary way.

Because I'm not writing a guide book I shall not give a step-by-step account of the route. I shall do what Dorothy did. The Wordsworths knew every rock, every tree and many spots were given family names or personal identities: John's grove, Sara's gate and so on. I shall go out with Dorothy in spirit and look at particular things in her uniquely personal way: using, where possible, her own words.

In attempting this I have to re-learn how to look at landscape. It is difficult in the Lakes not to be overwhelmed by the "grand scale". The sweep of landscape carries the eye far, rather than near. One mentally ticks off the names of the mountains: one admires the colours, the light and shade, the moving of cloud shadows across the fell side. Dorothy, of course, had eyes for the vista too. On Boxing Day 1801, whilst leaning over Sara's gate, she observes; "Grasmere Lake a beautiful image of stillness, clear as glass reflecting all things, the wind up and the waters sounding. The lake of a rich purple, the fields a soft yellow, the island yellowish-green, the copses red brown, the mountains purple. The church and buildings how quiet they were."

She is equally perceptive with the minutae of the pathways and walls. "Catkins are coming out; palm trees budding; the alder with its plumb coloured buds" all convey a restlessness on the part of nature. A kind of impatience that winter is not yet over and spring is being held back. Even in inclement weather the walk was taken: ". . . walked into Easedale, to gather mosses. It was piercing cold and a hailstorm came on in the afternoon".

In spring and summer the details become more precise. "I never saw daffodils so beautiful. They grew among the mossy stones about and about them; some rested their heads upon these stones as on a pillow for weariness; and the rest tossed and reeled and danced, and seemed as if they verily laughed with the wind . . ."

That undoubtedly was the origin of her brother's best known poem.

I could go on, stone by mossy stone; view upon view; chance glimpses of some swift living thing darting away. As I left the area the sun was low in the sky; the shadows long. I paused and looked across what is an undeniably beautiful view. Then a piece of shadow moved and detached itself. At first I thought it was a baby otter, a rare sighting. But otters don't climb trees.

It was a pine marten: and they are rarer still.

Them and Us

It is not advisable, when in the company of true Yorkshire folk, to mention that, between the fifth and eighth centuries, Yorkshire was part of the Saxon kingdom of Northumbria.

However, as any true native would be quick to point out, the Humber is the boundary between England and Yorkshire to the South. Therefore, it follows, that anything North (and West) of that demarcation must inevitable be North-Humber-Land and therefore Yorkshire proper or, at least, part of the huge Ebor Empire which ends at Hadrian's Wall northward and St Bee's Head to the west.

It is a country of abundance in every respect. Over many centuries, streams of citizens with enormous talent have gone forth to civilize the rest of the Christian World. They took with them culture, literature and customs that are nowadays universally enjoyed but not always acknowledged as to their origins.

Take the giving of Christmas presents fro example. It was started at York. Seriously. I'm not talking about the red-robed Santa with his whiskers and "Ho, Ho, Ho". That travesty is a wholly American invention: a strictly commercial enterprise.

Yorkshire Christmas — Old Christmas Day that is: January 6th — began around 200 AD when the Roman Emperor, Severus, resided in and ruled from York. Officers of rank and nobility were expected to present the Emperor with gifts like cake and honey to symbolise sweetness and gold. Until, that is, the Emperor realised that he was onto a good thing and demanded not symbolic gold but the real thing. Perhaps it was as well for all the officials that Severus's York reign lasted for just three years.

Still on the theme of culture and customs. It is amazing how many scholars of the early years of the first millennium, had their origins or their beginnings in this extreme North Eastern corner of Yorkshire.

Take, for example, Alcuin of York who flourished from 735 — 804. He was a scholar who travelled widely, visited Rome, advised the Holy Roman Emperor himself, Charlemagne the Great, and ended up as Abbot of the Monastery at Tours.

He also sustained the idea of hordes of scholars deriving from that northern outpost of culture by being severally known as Ealwine, Albinus or Ealhwine; depending, presumably upon which language you read him in.

Considerably less travelled; but equally revered by the "Victorian" school of spiritual history was Caedmon who flourished somewhat earlier than Alcuin. He, who was a simple cattle-minder, had a vision one night in which an angel commanded him to sing. This he did and when he came out of his visionary

73

state he found that he retained the art of singing: something he had never been able to do before. This miraculous gift enabled him to enter the monastic order at Whitby where he dedicated himself to praising God in poetry and song for the rest of his days.

I have mentioned already how Alcuin's name existed in many variations. He was not, of course, the only writer with nommes de plume. Mention John Holywood in mixed but scholarly company. From all but the most erudite you will likely get a blank stare. But gently drop the name Sacrobosco and you will get an instant response: argument and cross-argument, flourishing gestures and sounds. You will get references to "authorities" such as Lynn Thorndike, Ashworth Underwood and, of course, Charles Singer: historians and scholars every one.

Why is this? Because John Holywood and Sacrobosco were the same man. Little is known about John Holywood except that (as Sacrobosco) he died in Paris in 1250. One must assume that teaching in Paris, and being the author of the standard medieval textbook of astronomy, John Holywood was not anxious to broadcast the fact that he was born in Halifax. Don't get me wrong: Halifax has a lot going for it (including an outstanding hands-on museum called Eureka). I am very fond of Halifax but somehow one does not expect it to be the town which gave birth to a scholar whose Tractatus de Sphaera (or Sphaera mundi) went into some 230 editions, and was the standard work on the subject for hundreds of years.

Not least of its interest is the evidence that medieval scholars did not believe in a flat earth. As his title confirms, John Holywood (sorry — Sacrobosco) thought otherwise: and he got it direct from Ptolemy and the Arabs.

Maps have always fascinated me and I am grateful that the Mappa mundi — which has the then-known world centred upon Jerusalem — remains where it belongs: in Hereford Cathedral.

Would that an even older, manuscript map come to light after hundreds of years in hiding. It ought to be in York Minster by rights but nobody will even discuss it. Likewise with Ripon Cathedral and Beverley Minster, whose archivists deny any knowledge.

I am referring to the Carta Eboracum of course. This treasure remains hidden, probably where it was buried when Imperial Rome departed and the Vikings came.

Gathering information is a bit like researching a thesis about the Freemasons: a fragment here; a dropped hint there. This much I can reveal, but no more. The Carta Eboracum is very similar to the Mappa mundi. With one important exception:

It is centred upon York and not Jerusalem.

Education for All

Very many years ago I tried my hand at writing Science Fiction. My stories appeared in a magazine called New Worlds, which was edited by Michael Moorcock. Even in those days, and living as I was, surrounded by Pennine landscape, I was pessimistic about the future and I shared my disillusion with such writers as George Orwell and E.M. Forster. Now,forty or so years on, I still have waking nightmares along the lines of Forster's short story *The Machine Stops*. In it humans live underground in total physical isolation, in a honeycomb of cells, connected with the rest of humanity by electronic means only.

It is horribly like the "real world" in which everything; shopping, entertainment, education, is conducted over the net. The classroom gives way to the web; the pub defers to the chatroom. It is information without education.

I am not an intellectual Luddite. I do not look back to a golden age of warm human contacts with sentimental nostalgia. Life was tough; very tough. We had to struggle, but we did communicate. And our communications were tactile and personal, made by face to face relationship: and not through the impersonal steering and clicking of a sweaty electronic mouse far into the night.

Bit by bit this diatribe is coming round to the cause and effect of popular education. Official education of the compulsory kind began in the 1870s. It led to anger and resentment — especially amongst the farming community — but compulsory education, like the proverbial green bay tree, has continued to flourish.

The education I am thinking about is of voluntary learning for its own sake. Education for all; not simply for the wealthy or the clergy. The education given by the WEA — or local lecturing boards such as E.M. Forster taught for in 1906 — and, in the north, the Mechanics' Institutes. This essentially nineteenth century movement is referred to by contemporary writers such as the Brontës and it provided popular education and training for the workers who wished to "better themselves". By natural growth and evolution these Institutes became Technical Colleges which gave rise to the Yorkshire College, (which became Leeds University). This is where Arthur Ransome's father lectured in history — and in which city Arthur himself was born in 1884.

All of this suggests that there was a thirst for knowledge amongst working people. A thirst that went far beyond the obtaining of simple vocational skills. History and Politics; Classical Art and Mythology; Biblical History and Literature were all on offer and in demand.

But as the curriculum of state education broadened out, "popular education" became split into the vocational and political on the one hand and the private literary and debating societies on the other. And this is where I came in.

For several years, back in the late fifties and early sixties, I lectured for the Association of Yorkshire Bookmen. I can't remember how I became involved in the first place but I think I was recommended to put my name forward by a scholarly and impassioned believer in popular culture, called Frank Beckwith.

I do not know just how widespread the Association was. My own circuit was a close knit itinerary around the Heavy Woollen District of the West Riding; plus a trip out to Skipton on occasions. I can't remember now the full range of topics on each individual society's annual list. But it was wide in its choice from local history, international literature, literary memoirs and topics in popular linguistics such as place names or dialects. Meetings were either held in parish halls or schools or, on rare occasions, in the committee rooms of pubs. Payment was not generous but adequate and refreshment varied from the typical Yorkshire high tea to a full blown meal of generous dimensions. It was always "an occasion"; not simply educational, but social and always welcoming.

Each society was autonomous where choice of subjects was concerned and methods of invitation varied from a chosen listing, from which a speaker could choose, or by selection and submission of subjects by individual speakers.

For myself, I usually put forward my own suggestion. I usually spoke about my favourite literary topics — diarists, contemporary novelists or children's literature. But it was out of a casual conversation, almost a chance remark, that I was invited to speak at Brighouse on a topic involving place names. Because the suggestion was made at the end of a meeting, I had a whole year to ponder the subject and research it. At that time the subject was relatively unfamiliar to me but as I studied and researched the interest grew into what is now a linguistic passion.

It would not be appropriate to reproduce here the full text of the talk. In any case, it was given from rather sketchy notes. However, here are those notes, fleshed out and turned into real sentences. It may provide some idea of a fascinating evening. We must always remember that communication is a two-way process from which I gained immensely during the question and answer session that followed.

Celtic River Names.

Most of us who are middle-aged and more will remember the Geographical mnemonic SUNWAC.

These are the Dales rivers that flow eastward across the Pennines and end up joining the Yorkshire Ouse making its independent way to the North Sea. From the north and travelling south, the rivers are Swale, Ure, Nidd, Wharfe, Aire and Calder. Four of these names, along with the Ouse and the Esk, can all be traced back to Celtic origins. (Only the Wharfe and the Swale do not.) And, moreover, these names in some form or another are repeated all over the land.

Because I know the Yorkshire landscape best I shall deal with Yorkshire rivers. But it must be said that areas which have a Celtic heritage (Cornwall, Wales and Scotland, for example) have many more rivers whose names have changed little, if at all, over thousands of years.

First there are the names which had the general meaning of "water" or "stream". Although not represented in Yorkshire, the river name Avon is possibly the best known example. The modern Welsh word for river is, in fact, afon. Northern examples are Esk, Ouse and Don. There is, of course, an Exe in Devon, Ouses in Sussex and the Midlands and, (extending our boundaries somewhat), the Danube. Esk has a Celtic origin in Isca, Ouse in Usso and Don in Dana

Leven (or Levens) occurs in Yorkshire, Cumbria and Scotland. It is both place name and river name. It derives from Leuan and Leuan was a Celtic water nymph. So far we have dealt with names that derive from Celtic words that show a general association with water.

Far more interesting and enlightening are the names which have a specific derivation. Having lived and worked for many years in what used to be called the Heavy Woollen District I am interested to learn that Calder (Caled in origin) means hard and swift and Aire, which derives from Isara, is strong.

Having also lived for a time near Bedale it was interesting to discover that the River Ure (from Isura) means swift and also that it has a linguistic association with the Isar, a tributary of the Danube. The list goes on and the language becomes more revealing.

Derwent, which derives from derua and means oak tree, appears on several regional maps. Dove also, from the Celtic dubo for black or dark is something of a puzzle to any one who knows the bright beauty of Derbyshire's Dovedale. Yet, even today, the Gaelic word for dark is dubh and it occurs in many landscape or place names , especially in the Highlands & Islands. Another Celtic word for dark is tam. This appears in Yorkshire and elsewhere as Tame (there is a Tame in Oxfordshire for example) and, of course, Thames.

Finally, let us emerge from this darkness into the fresh, bright newness of Nouijos, for that is the Celtic word for such radiance. Again, as a river name, it is widespread today. Yorkshire has the Nidd, that glorious river of sparkling waters and swift grayling, and Wales has the Neath, which in Welsh is Newydd.

Where does all this get us? In practical terms not very far. But in terms of getting to know our origins, how our ancestors saw themselves and the places they lived in, a very great way indeed. And if this short piece does no more than whet the appetite for more curiosity about where we live and the world about us, then it will have done a good thing.

A Different Kind of Landmark

Pen-y-ghent, when we lived in the Ribblesdale area, was not just a landmark. It was the focal point of our existence.

When people came to visit us from afar it was Pen-y-ghent that we told them to "home in" on before giving them more specific directions.

When we moved further south, into a landscape of moorland rather than scarrs and fells, we had to find a different kind of landmark. There really was no choice. From whichever point of the compass we travelled, the only feature that signalled our homecoming was man-made: Emley Moor TV Mast.

That such a grotesque symbol of modernness and electronic technology should be so compulsive a symbol to me — a dyed-in-the-wool countryman — might seem strange. But it was not what it was, or represented, that drew me. It was by association that I grew, if not to love it, to make it the symbol of a certain way of life. In fact, even now, when I think of Emley mast I think first of sheep dog trials, hunter-chases and team-chases, and then of haymaking, baling and leading the bales into a Dutch barn. Let me explain.

For most of the time that we lived thereabouts we had a farm cottage: a very old farm cottage. It was attached to a farm that was at least 250 years old and had once — in pre-industrial Revolution times — been a textile centre of the cottage weaving industry. We lived in what had then been the weaving shed, although shed is a slightly misleading name for a gritstone dwelling with walls several feet thick.

In our day the farm was essentially a livestock/ grazing farm and much of it was given over to a livery stable where several horses were kept and used both for hacking and riding to hounds with the Rockwood Harriers.

We were both otherwise occupied (teaching and lecturing) and by this time the children had grown up and left home, therefore we became closely involved in the farm and stables. It was inevitable since country life was always our choice, if not our vocation. And although we both had to travel some miles to work we were in no way commuters seeking the best of both worlds. In any case, everything that is memorable about those days, and worth recording, all happened within sight of Emley mast which is why — even today — I feel a flood of emotion when travelling northwards up the M1 and count the miles north of Sheffield before it comes into view.

The mast that we literally looked up to was a tall, slender cylinder — allegedly the tallest unsupported structure in Europe when it was built. It was not, however, the mast that was there originally. That was a very different kind of structure supported by thick tension cables. One night in a fierce gale the mast blew down. The cables broke, and one of them sliced in two the village chapel as it fell. At the very time it happened there was a woman inside cleaning and making the place ready for Sunday. She escaped unscathed.

Amazingly there were no human casualties at all. The event was little more than a nine-day wonder (except for the nearest residents), but people did travel many miles to visit the site and to exercise their imaginations as to the circumstances.

The present structure is also visited and it has open days. People who have been to the observation area at the top are astounded by the view. They are also somewhat put out by the degree of swing that can be felt, especially on a breezy day.

Being a dedicated coward where such things are concerned, and knowing that lightning can strike twice in the same place, I prefer to rely on hearsay.

Animal Hospital at Home

We take central heating, bathrooms and similar amenities very much for granted these days. It was not always the case, although I strenuously deny the slander that mill workers, miners and similar ever assumed that the bath was for storing coal! That was put about by Punch magazine and music hall comedians.

I can, however, vouch for two instances when our bath was used for, shall we say, unorthodox habits — although on a very temporary basis in each case.

It would have been some time in the early 1970s. We had an Afghan hound. This, in itself, was a domestic liability but to compound the issue we had her simultaneously with Mungo, the Irish setter. Cleo — that was her family name — was everything that Afghans are reputed to be: imperious, playful, incredibly loyal to one person, and their devotion is absolute.

The passionate aspect would have been troublesome with a full blooded Irish setter in the family: (and, the result of a stray meeting between the two beggared the imagination!). Neutering was the only way out. We tossed a coin and Mungo won. We booked in Cleo to be spayed.

She came back from the surgery somewhat subdued; but not for long. She was back to her old tricks of tormenting Mungo and playing off one human member of the family against another.

She had been shaved and in the heat of July the shaven area must have been sore. We tried a soothing cream but that didn't work. She simply licked it off and made herself sick. In the end, she solved the problem herself. Not only whilst the skin was sore and red but even after the hair had grown again, Cleo spent all her days and nights lying in the bath (without water of course) pressing her shorn underparts against the cool ceramic surface. It solved the problem for Cleo, but it was a difficult job getting her out, if anyone wanted a bath when she was in residence.

The other time when our bath was used for alternative purposes is bizarre. Without the photograph my wife thoughtfully took, I would find it hard, some twenty-five years later, to believe that it ever happened. For obvious reasons this incident did not coincide with Cleo's reign.

Some time during the evening I would take Mungo for a walk. It was almost the same route every time but it was varied enough always to find something interesting to see or to do. Part of the route was across a defunct brickyard, around a pond which held carp of legendary size, and back onto a road which then led to a side road and a circle back to home.

I cannot understand even now why it happened, but it did. We had gone round the pond and crossed the field and were just about to cross the road. It was dusk but not dark. Mungo came suddenly alert, froze in his tracks and pointed, as only a setter or pointer can point, at a huddled object by the road side.

I was used to Mungo's points. Being a frustrated gun dog he would point at anything. His usual point was to freeze elegantly, stiffen his tail and go forward onto his front legs and push his muzzle in the direction of his real (or imaginary) prey. He then flared his nostrils and snorted.

This was a different kind of point. It was more wary and the snorting had an excited edge to it. We both approached the huddled object. We were both accustomed to creatures struck by cars; rabbits, foxes and sometimes badgers. Mungo gave them barely a glance.

This was different. This was an exhausted but still living great crested grebe. There, at the side of a road from Huddersfield to Sheffield. It was still alive but weak. Wary of its dagger-like beak, I cradled it in my sweater and we all went home.

What could we do? To start with we used a large cardboard box and kept it warm with a light bulb. We tried tempting the bird with bits of raw herring with no success. However, bit by bit it rallied. Who had the bright idea first I do not know but we filled the bath with tepid water and gently put the bird into the bath. It struggled feebly, but it swam.

Then my daughter had a brilliant idea. After consulting a bird book she emptied the contents of an aquarium containing tadpoles into the bath. By the time the RSPCA arrived to collect it, the bird had perked up no end and was even "diving" for tadpoles.

The whole of the time the grebe was in the house, Mungo watched with his "puzzled setter" expression.

The grebe must have strayed from the pond nearby. It may have been making for the stream across the road and lost its nerve. It was one of the highlights of our time in that home. In those days grebes were rare anywhere except on the Norfolk Broads. It was a quarter of a century ago and the bird is long dead. But it feels good to confer some kind of immortality even after all these years.

The Young Pigs in The Dale

In a sense I brought it on myself. I was listening-in to a conversation at the next table. It was Leyburn. It was market day and it seemed as if the whole of Wensleydale had moved in for the occasion.

"Aye: if 'e coom once, 'e coom a dozen times. A right Grisedale pie it were."

This assertion, delivered with all the Dalesman's conviction and bluntness drew my attention at once. I was working on an idea at the time for writing, not a dialect dictionary, but a book of idiomatic words and phrases covering the whole of the north. I had accumulated dozens of expressions that varied from dale to dale. and area to area, which nevertheless expressed common ideas.

This was a new one to me: Grisedale Pies. Before I had time to make contact the elderly couple had paid up and gone. I tried to be logical about it; linguistic even. The Grisedale bit was the easiest. Grisedale (with either "s" or "z") is fairly common in Cumbria and the High Pennines. It derives from the Old Norse. Griss + dael the dale (or valley) of the young pigs. Therefore, so my logic told me, we were dealing with

Grisedale pies — that is pork pies from a place called Grisedale.

It was really too simple; hardly worth taking note. I did, however, ask around one or two people who were interested in language and dialect. But short of having my etymology confirmed I got no closer to what the phrase meant idiomatically. I came to a total dead end. So much so that I went about my day to day business and shelved the matter.

And then, as so often happens; I heard the expression used once more. This time it was at the sheep auction in Hawes.

"Yon tup's been int'market a dozen times. Back and foorth like a Grised'l Pie."

The farmer was talking about a particular Swaledale tup which seemed to find getting a permanent home something of a problem. For all its majestic appearance, there was something about that tup which brought it back for sale time and again. It may have been a rogue tup on the fell side — an "escape artist" for example or it might not have been good at its job of getting ewes into lamb. Whatever the case it did the rounds of all the sheep markets from Teesdale to Nidderdale and back again.

I simply had to ask. The conversation went something like this:

"I'm sorry to interrupt, but that tup."

"Aye."

"You just called it a Grisedale Pie".

"Aye." [It was hard going for me]

"I know most shepherding words, but that's a new one. Can you let on?"

"Aye. A Grised'l Pie's what we call summat as turns up again and again. Like a bad penny you'd say."

So that was that. Nothing more than a casual expression to denote someone who comes often and outstays his welcome. But why Grisedale? Nobody knew. I even went to Grisedale hamlet high up at the head of Wensleydale but got nowhere.

I even wondered if the pie might have been an exceptionally indigestible one which stuck in the gullet as well as the mind. I even let my literary imagination loose upon the subject and remembered an entry in my beloved *Diary of Parson Woodforde*: "mince pie rose oft." Could this be the reason for it?

By this time my curiosity was overwhelming. Outside Wensleydale the expression was unknown, or seemed to be. In the dale itself several older people knew what it meant, as an idiom that is; but no-one knew why.

Eventually I ran it to earth by accident in a secondhand bookshop in Richmond. I was looking through the books of local history and travel. On a low shelf, next to Wordsworth's *Guide to the Lakes* was a *Guide to Wensleydale* by John Routh. I was looking through it when, almost by chance, I came upon this paragraph.

"A potato pie was once made in Grisedale and, being forgotten, was not brought out for half a year, when the potatoes are said to have taken root, and grown out at the top of the crust. The pie was frequently afterwards placed upon the table, but nobody seemed fond of it."

As I said at the beginning: I brought it on myself really.

The Road to Hardraw Force

Although it was never central in my life, I have always had a soft spot for Hawes. For some of our time in the Dales we lived just off Ribblesdale and used to visit Hawes as an alternative to Settle. For the rest of the time we lived near Bedale, considerably to the east of Hawes, which is high up at the head of Wensleydale and the meeting place of many highways and trackways.

Our usual way home from Hawes took us up Ribblesdale to Ribblehead (which appears elsewhere in these memoirs) and across the gloriously named Blea Moor, Gayle moor and Widdale Fell. And it is along that lonely road, about four miles on from Ribblehead, that we passed our favourite building. No, not the building itself but its potential and its location. The building was possibly a shepherd's dwelling, or a shippon. It is not a traditional Dales barn and it is only one storey high.

Set on a spit of land near to a beck, it has glorious views of fell and dale on all sides. The bonus is the view that it has of Pen-y-ghent to the south-east. A prospect unequalled in all Yorkshire! It is a dwelling of fantasy.

Using windpower and solar panels; taking water from the beck and installing caravan-style sanitation; one could live there all the year round, with good ventilation in the summer and a wood-burning stove for winter. In fact, one could modify the stove to burn peat (readily available thereabouts) and be virtually independent of "civilization". One would have to buy food and clothing of course but with the inevitable mobile phone life could be lived on one's own terms. And in all probability one would be more aware of one's neighbours — seen as sparkles of light on a dark night, from across miles of fell — than in the tree lined streets of a suburb.

* * *

I do not know even now whether Hawes is a town or just a big village. It matters not: there is a good street market and a superb auction mart for sheep. What more does a place need to justify its existence in that bleak but glorious spot which has managed to attract the attention (and retain the affection) of a number of writers and artists.

Two, in particular, separated by something like 150 years, must stand as representatives of all the others who remain unmentioned but not unknown. Neither was native of Yorkshire but both were Northerners of that special kind who had a distinct individuality coupled with an uncanny ability to "see the other fellow's point of view" in a totally unsentimental way. One was William Wordsworth, who passed through Hawes in

1799 en route for Grasmere with sister Dorothy; the other, a frequent visitor, was a vet from Thirsk called Alfie Wight; better known as James Herriot.

Wordsworth must have done the journey many times. After all, Hawes is on the main Sedbergh to Leyburn road (though only a rough track in Wordsworth's time) and he must have travelled it from Grasmere, when he lived at Dove Cottage, to East Yorkshire and into Teesdale, on many occasions.

The only journey that interests us here is the one he and Dorothy made in December 1799. The Wordsworths stopped off at Hawes and made a point of visiting Hardraw Force. Not only that, the great man wrote a letter to his close friend Coleridge, four days after arriving at Dove Cottage on Christmas Eve. Hardraw Force made a lasting impression on both of them.

Wordsworth's description of Hardraw Force is worth reading in its entirety. But the passages that describe the actual cascade impressed me most because I, too, have seen the place on a winter's day under similar conditions. ". . . the water which shot from the extreme height of the fall (seemed) to be dispersed before it reached the bason, into a thin shower of snow that was tossed about like snow blown from the roof of a house." Then, having reached the actual fall itself, ". . . over stones of all colours and sizes encased in the clearest ice formed by the spray of the waterfall, we found the rock which before had seemed a perpendicular wall extending itself over us like the ceiling of a huge cave." The whole spot, once you get through the entry point — which in true Yorkshire fashion is a paying turnstile in a pub! — contains an air of mystery and almost of magic. I sensed it just as the Wordsworths did and the shivers were not entirely to do with the cold. James Herriot, who visited it in bright sunshine, felt it too and described the place as "eerie".

As far as the Wordsworths were concerned the entire journey was made through bitter cold with the wind driving the snow behind them. William and Dorothy were the 29 and 28 years old respectively and were making the journey of some 100 miles over-all, in late December. What is more, they were doing it on foot (except for occasionally hitch hiking on farm carts). Having experienced many a Dales winter myself, their strength and stamina astound me.

I wrote above that Hawes is the meeting place of many highways and trackways. And so it is. The Wordsworths took the highway out towards Sedbergh and on to Kendal and Grasmere (having already travelled the same road since Richmond). James Herriot was most impressed by the way out which is called the Buttertubs Pass. This is a precipitous track that leads up and over the heads of the dales and into Swaledale to the north. He did it at least once on foot (when Youth hostelling with his children) and also by car "for business reasons".

As a family we approached Hawes from a completely different direction. In fact, when the family were teenagers, we did it almost as a ritual and certainly as a challenge.

Every New Year's Day — the snowier the better — we began our journey at Buckden, far up the relatively "civilized" Wharfedale. We then set off, suitably equipped with flasks of coffee, chocolate bars and Kendal mint cake, to drive over the high fells to Hawes via such Scandinavian named places as Hubberholme, Beckermonds, Outershaw and Gayle. Most years the trip was exhilarating and exciting. Occasionally it was scary (especially for a daughter who has always experienced agoraphobia away from shopping precincts and malls!)

Only once in several years did we have to give up and return the way we began. At the highest point of the pass there was such a blizzard that even my wife, who as a driver would normally cope with everything, accepted defeat. And even then she wanted to go round to Hawes by an easier route and see if we could get to the "turnback point" from the other end. Eventually we did turn back: after some rather exciting moments manoeuvring the car on a single track road with a precipitous drop on the near-side (a good job the afore-mentioned daughter didn't know about that at the time!)

What slightly spoiled an otherwise exciting day out was the churlish behaviour of the landlord of the pub at Buckden who, in spite of our obvious travel stained state, refused us any kind of refreshment whatsoever and even begrudged us the use of the toilets on the grounds that "it's out of hours".

In much more recent times Hawes has seen a resurgence of an industry that almost died out: the making of Wensleydale cheese. This exquisite cheese, which all true Yorkshire folk eat with Christmas cake, was first made from ewes' milk by the monastic farmers. It then changed from sheep's milk to cows' milk and was then made on farms and sold from gates as well as from Hawes market until quite recently. As demand grew the manufacture was centralised at a creamery in Hawes. This venture endured mixed fortunes. The final indignity came when the parent company tried to close the creamery altogether and transfer the whole business of making Wensleydale cheese to Lancashire!

The workforce rose up in justifiable rebellion and bought out the company to be run on co-operative lines. This began a turnabout of fortune. The public were invited in to demonstrations, a tourist shop was opened and a café was built to provide for the coach parties that visited from far and wide.

Not least of the fortunes was the sponsorship — if that is the right word — of Nick Park. His endearing characters, of many award winning films, boosted the sale of Wensleydale cheese to levels hitherto unimaginable. I have no doubt that any mention of Wallace and Gromit almost anywhere in the world will produce an instant reference to cheese; Wensleydale, of course.

How Daft Can You Get?

High up in the Dale there is a village school which has escaped closure. Its twenty or so pupils still benefit by not being bussed to the nearest town. It may be unique (who can tell?) but it is certainly unusual in that its two teachers are mother and daughter.

Mother provides the continuity. She has taught two generations of many of the fell farm families. She plays the kind of role in that scattered community that the old fashioned matron did to the pre-Trust hospitals. Daughter is intelligent, imaginative and lacking in worldly ambition. When she was not teaching, Susie was out and about sketching and painting. Her work sold too, mainly to the makers of greetings cards, and many tourists left with examples of her work from the gallery of the local tea shop.

It was May Day and a school holiday. Up and down the Dale activities were being done to celebrate the real start of the tourist season. Farms were open to visitors, village halls became temporary craft centres, schools provided all kinds of entertainment of the "what life was like when Grannie was a girl" style with Victorian costumes and old fashioned cooking and ancient household utensils.

Susie and her mother provided a novel kind of entertainment. Susie gave an on-going masterclass for aspiring dales artists and mother had the children for a different kind of hands-on activity. She organised — after careful research — a "children's games down the ages" display.

I watched entranced but the sound was deafening. Susie joined us as we watched, taking time out from her masterclass.

"Here she is," said her mother. "The true creator of the idea."

"Not at all, mother." She turned to me. "I simply showed her Breugel's painting 'Children's games' and left the rest to her."

As we watched, a solitary child with an intense expression was trying to carry a jar full of water on her head. This was obviously inspired by an illustration from a children's Bible of Pharaoh's daughter and her maidens. At least, that's what Susie suggested.

Two paces, a perilous wobble, and down crashed the jar showering the girl with water. As mother dashed forward to assist, Susie turned to me with a grin and said — in an exaggerated accent — "Aye, daft as a brush that one." I agreed and thought no more of the incident until suddenly, later that evening, I wondered to myself "why daft as a brush"? Why should a brush be daft? Yet it is a common expression of exasperated despair throughout the North of England.

I asked my wife: she didn't know why. I asked friends with a flair for language. Eventually I got in touch with someone in the Yorkshire Dialect Society.

Apparently it is just one of a number of expressions all similarly comparing a rather stupid or clumsy person with a common tool or utensil. "Daft as a yat (i.e. a gate)" is one such, "daft as a wagon-horse" is another. The general opinion is that any creature or object that does the roughest or toughest or dirtiest job is "daft". Hence the connections.

One variant comes from the Lake District. "Daft as a swill." None of us knew what a swill is. And after several years of asking, I still don't know.

Morning Light

Coming, as I do, from Norfolk it seems perfectly reasonable to me that I should be fascinated by mountains. I remember vividly, whilst still in the sixth form, the first publication of *Mountaineering in Scotland* by W. H. Murray. I could not afford to buy a copy, but being a school librarian I was able to recommend it as a useful purchase.

It was some thirty years later that I got round to buying a copy. It is not exactly a constant literary companion but I have read it many times and will go on doing so even though my "days on the hill" are long past.

By means of that book I have vicariously climbed every notable Scottish peak and ridge. Only once have I ever tried to emulate "the master" and that was not either Highlands or Islands, but Ingleborough. which at the time was almost literally my next door neighbour.

My favourite chapter in Murray's book tells the story of how a group of close climbing companions climbed Ben Nevis on New Year's Eve and saw in the New Year from a tent. Together they endured a difficult night, trying to balance warmth with ventilation in their tent, but were rewarded by a dawn of incredible beauty as the rising sun lit up every Highland peak for miles; all of them snowbound. The culmination of the pre-dawn palette of every shade of rose and orange was the blinding appearance of the sun which turned to gold everything it touched.

That was the high point. The midnight moment was very much a subdued affair, the celebration being a shared mug of Mummary's blood. This is a concoction beloved by members of the Scottish Mountaineering Club. It consists of a combination of Rum and Bovril served as hot as possible: very sustaining I believe.

My own adventure was very low key when compared to my hero's. To start with, my wife heard me out in total silence. Then: "Well, if you're daft enough to do that, you'll do it on your own. I'll not join you and I doubt if anyone else will either."

She was right of course.

Kitted out with very-cold-weather gear and a high altitude tent, I set off. My trusty rucksack crammed with everything I could pack in that I might need. It included Mountaineering in Scotland.

My wife's parting words were designed to comfort and encourage. "You'd be wise to set off in good time. You don't want to be messing about on Simon Fell at nightfall do you?" De-coded this meant: "Make sure you get up before dark, with your navigational skills you could end up anywhere."

Her precise final comment was: "If you're not back by lunch time tomorrow I'll get the Fell Rescue out."

The route up was tedious to say the least. Ingleborough is nothing if not a slog up over gritstone fell and limestone pavement. The summit plateau looked uninviting and faintly dusted with snow. I chose my site with care. This wasn't simply a prudent examination of the terrain. It was putting off the critical moment of setting up the tent as long as possible.

Putting up a tent on ground that is frozen to a depth of several inches is an activity designed to keep one warm — even if the air was blue for much of the time. I set up camp, I brewed coffee and followed this with a nourishing meal of freeze-dried paella. It was now quite dark. I switched the stove unit for a lantern on the gaz cylinder and lay down to read Mountaineering in Scotland. I must have dozed off because I became suddenly aware that the wind had got up. The tent was billowing but it stayed intact.

I struggled into my boots and my duvet coat and went outside. I walked around the desolate summit trying to summon up something of the elation felt by W. H. Murray and his friends on that pioneering night. I failed and most ignominiously I put on the stove, boiled water for coffee and, I confess it, filled the hot water bottle that my wife had sardonically slipped into the outer pocket of my rucksack. Bless her!

From then on things went wrong. Well, not exactly wrong: not according to plan. I fell asleep and woke at 12.30 a.m. I'd missed seeing in the New Year. What is more, I could no longer get to sleep. I lay with the tent door open and surveyed the unimpressive scene.

I was so lonely. If a passing rabbit, or a mountain hare or even a weasel or stoat had appeared I would have invited it into the tent for company. But nothing stirred. I re-lit the stove and used the previous water to re-heat the hot water bottle and, frankly, felt sorry for myself.

Then it happened. Tentatively at first there were lights on the horizon. Lights that crept higher into the sky. It was like a silent storm, lightning but no thunder. And what lightning it was. Sheet lightning, forked lightning, lightning of every shade and hue. The entire spectrum flared before me. I was enthralled.

I had seen the Northern Lights before from the deck of a cruising yacht in Balvicar Bay. That had been impressive. This was spectacular. It begged description and I didn't even have a camera to retain it.

It passed as suddenly as it began. The sun came up. It was not the spectacular sunrise that Murray described. It was rather mundane to be honest. But what I had experienced was a magical display that aroused in me all the atavistic overtones of a romantic nature.

Almost anything else would be an anticlimax. I packed up my tent and gear and returned to earth. I was home long before lunch time and I was unusually silent about my experiences.

Until I'd had a bath and a well cooked meal that is. Then I could hold it in no longer.

Scalin Muck

Fifty or so years ago, schools high up in the dales villages were almost self governing. Being remote from the County Council Education Department in Skipton meant a visit from the C.C. inspector twice yearly at most. The quality of the school therefore reflected the quality of the head teacher.

Alfred Mason — Alf to his friends and Alf also to all his pupils behind his back — was a jewel of a man. A born teacher, younger son of a sheep farmer from back o' Skiddaw, he fitted easily into his task of guiding and teaching not only the village children but those, too, from remote farms. Although Cumbrian rather than Dalesman, Alf spoke their language and understood their calendar. And despite his degree in English, he was most at home in the company of farmers and shepherds. He was strong on discipline, and a good listener and to hear him telling the legends and stories of the North Country was to be transported into the world of fantasy and held there by the power of the word alone.

Alf was particularly respected for his understanding of the needs of the family farm. At times of pressure or crisis such as lambing or haytiming and such like, he accepted the absences from school of farm pupils without complaint, so long as time was made up to compensate. And such was the in-built sense of fair play in all dalesfolk, time was, indeed, made up.

Then suddenly, on a weekend in the early part of the year, Alf had a stroke. Not a seriously disabling and humiliating stroke but serious enough to affect both sight and speech. He took retirement and on a short-term, almost a supply basis, a stop gap head was appointed until the formalities of appointing a substantive head were completed.

And so it was that Mardale school found itself at the mercy of a totally inappropriate temporary head. Yes, he was academically sound and yes, he could certainly teach. He was an administrator par excellence and he was clearly destined for control of one of the, at that time, newly created urban comprehensives. In that he would (indeed he did) succeed. At Mardale he simply did not even try to understand what motivates the family of a farmer.

Worst of all he was strict about attendance. Neither lambing nor leading hay, in his eyes, ought to excuse a boy from school. It was this obdurate attitude that led, in the end, to a confrontation which at the outset persuaded him that he just didn't belong. What happened eventually is another story.

At registration on Monday morning he put an absence against the name of Nicky Stansgate of High Foss Farm. It was one of a number of zeros that decorated the line against Nicky's name. In all his nine years as a scholar, Nicky had only rarely completed a full week. In Stansgate eyes the absences were fully justified — "workin' on t'farm". By Wednesday Robert Marshall (the temporary head) began asking questions of the class. There was no attempt at dissimulation, no thought of covering up what to all the boys was a perfectly legitimate — even a legal — reason for absence.

"'E's working on' t'farm, mister."

"Aye, 'e's scalin muck in t'medder."

"He's doing what?" Robert Marshall was clearly out of his depth.

"Scalin muck".

Eventually he worked out from more graphic details that Nicky was spreading manure evenly over the meadow land to stimulate the grass for hay.

"Go up and see for thissen, sir." This suggestion was echoed by others whose imaginations were influenced by the thought of the meticulously dressed townee going anywhere near the stockyard of a Dales farmer.

"Aye," added a voice from the back of the class, "but tek thi wellies wi' thee."

And that is exactly what Robert Marshall did. The following afternoon he drove up the long, curving, cattle-gridded road that seemed to end in a midden. he was greeted noisily by two collies which prowled suspiciously around his car.

The noise of the dogs did two things. It alerted Nicky who was spreading the evenly spaced heaps of manure over the meadow with a rhythmical swing and a fluttering of the long tined fork.

"'Ello, sir, come to give a 'and?"

Before he had time to answer there came out from the farm house Nicky's older sister who had only just got in from her weekly trip to Settle market. At 23, she still lived at home and had a reputation for being a "sharp tongued 'un".

What happened next no one has ever been able to explain. The truth of the matter is probably pure accident, although for a long time Robert Marshall was certain that he'd been set up. Anyway at the sound of Katie's voice the two collies sped away just as Robert took a step forward towards Nicky. He tripped and fell at full stretch straight onto a heap of muck — farmyard manure at its very ripest.

As it happens it was, possibly, the best thing that could have occurred. Robert met Katie; who took him indoors and helped him to clean up. Nicky persuaded him that his absence was legitimate (his father being laid up by lumbago.). And Robert left some time later with a bucket of the same manure to put on his roses.

Obviously he had to return the bucket and so he made the second of several trips back up to the farm.

In time he kept a pair of wellies and a suit of dungarees in the boot of his car — just in case lumbago should once again afflict his future father-in-law.

Mice and Men

It was just a small and simple village bring and buy sale: to pay the ground rent for the scout hut for the next five years, or something like that. But what I was holding in my hands (hands that shook slightly from emotion) was a simple fruit bowl. It was broad and deep and might easily grace the High Table of an Oxbridge college. It had a functional simplicity and because of a combination of age and cherished polishing the oak grain seemed to ripple when it was moved or turned.

What really excited me was the tiny carved mouse that peeped up and over the rim. That said it all. The bowl was a genuine Robert Thompson piece, carved, as always, from a single chunk of perfectly seasoned oak. The fact that the mouse was an intrinsic part of the piece, and not carved separately and glued on, was all the provenance necessary.

Robert Thompson, the mouseman, was born at Kilburn in 1876. For all his working life he and his descendants, and his apprentices down to this day, worked as craftsmen, using traditional hand tools, creating great furniture and glorious artifacts from properly seasoned oak: always in oak. Always in oak?

Well, now I know of at least one exception: there may be more.

For about twenty-five years my wife taught at a Prep school. From small beginnings, the school, founded by Mr & Mrs Wilson grew and flourished. It then moved to a very large house that had once been the home of a Yorkshire wool baron.

On the lawn in front of this house, alongside the drive there grew an imposing willow tree. This tree must have had some very personal associations with the Wilsons because when the tree was eventually brought down in a gale, Mr Wilson had the tree carefully cut up and seasoned. He then, using his considerable powers of persuasion, set to work on Robert Thompson (whom he knew already). What inducements he used remain a secret to this day: but it worked. Mrs Wilson, in due course, became the owner of a Robert Thompson table, complete with mouse, but in willow not in oak. Remarkable! Times changed and the school passed into other hands. The table, however, was personal property and could not possibly have been on the school inventory. All this must have happened at least fifty years ago; in fact, Robert Thompson died in 1955. I wonder where the table is now?

I was thinking about all this as I stood and turned the simple fruit bowl in my hands. It was a simple tale; no drama, no family feuds, no questioned ownership: a simple tale about a man's gift to his wife. I wondered then what the fruit bowl would tell me if it could talk.

"That's a very nice piece you're holding there sir," the local vicar in charge of the stall. "Very nice indeed. Might I ask you £10 for it?"

What do you think?

And the Waters Covered The Earth

Even before the Saxons came there had been a Trod; a trackway that followed the line and curve of the gritstone edge. A droving road.

At a convenient point an intake was made and a crude structure — drystone and slate roofed — was put up for man and beast alike.

This was the first barn; part shippon, part human dwelling. What later generations would call a cote or coit. Strictly speaking it wasn't a barn at all, not in the sense of a "bere-aern" or Barley house. This was no settlement with small fields of barley, sickle-cut by hand and battered into submission by flails on the threshing stead.

No! This was intended for more transitory matters — a shelter against whatever nature chose to throw along with a "mew" for storing hay.

The actual incumbents are recorded neither by legend nor inscription. Exactly how many generations stretched through unrecorded time, from the first tentative attempts at permanency, to the time when the settlement (for so it became) was taken over by a monastic order are unknown to us.

And so it remained; an anonymous and unprepossessing cote until the time of Henry VIII, when it was sold off, entered a different phase altogether and passed into recorded history.

It became Newsteads. Whether the dwelling took its name from the family or vice versa I do not know. What is certain is that from the 17th century right up to the present time — the time towards which this preamble inevitably points — there has always been a Newstead living there. The male line without interruption. Not even a break of in-law occupation.

The Newsteads, almost by default, became fell farmers — livestock: mainly sheep with a house cow and a handful of bullocks. For this reason the cote remained intact; without modification. A continuous roof above the human and animal quarters. That is, for year after year.

But, bit by bit, generations of Newsteads undertook modifications and made improvements. A judicious use of mortar sealed the structure from the searing winds. The large stone hearth was modified. Where the fire had burned almost continuously, its peaty smoke drifting upwards towards a hole in the roof, now became a central fire of a different kind. A chimney was built as a channel for the smoke and a wall was built across the dwelling, cutting the space into bedroom and living room — separate but served by the same, ever burning, mound of peat. Later further divisions were made and a fotheringay, or passage, linked them all to the rear.

113

* * *

The twentieth century, in a mere fifty years, brought more changes than the previous 500. Paraffin lamps and stoves preceded electricity and calor gas. The road that had been a mere trackway was metalled and given a number on a map.

Chummy, the pony, began an honourable — and well earned — retirement and the little cart gradually fell apart.

The Newsteads always produced a son who was willing to take over in due time. In the staunchly non-conformist tradition he was always given a Biblical name. Something suitably Old Testament at first — Amos, Jude or even Seth — but this mellowed as time went on into the New Testament of Peter, Paul, Andrew or Mark.

The break with tradition came in 1950 when a curiously enlightened Maria Newstead after 20 fruitless years of marriage, prevailed upon her husband Stephen. Their eldest son — indeed, their only child — was duly named Nigel Newstead: Nigel Elvis Newstead to be precise.

And so it was: the first crack in the fabric of Newsteads. The first selfish, bookish, whey-faced little Newstead captivated his mother and alienated his father.

Which brings us up to date. Nigel grew from selfish childhood to selfish adulthood. Following a "nothing is too good for our Nigel" childhood we saw an "educated out of his station" young man (his father's words, not mine) who not only turned his back on farming but went to law instead. Quite literally: he became a lawyer specialising in conveyancing.

Whether Maria Newstead ever regretted what she had done "all for the best" as she thought or whether she remained defiantly maternal cannot be said for certain.

Certainly, after she became widowed, Maria lived on in solitude at Newsteads, renting out the land and living in an ever diminishing space that became, towards the end, bed-sitting-kitchen accommodation. Maria and Sam — the equally aged collie — lived with dignity. She accepted gifts of food but not as charity. She paid her way. And about once a month she had a visit from Nigel who helped to organise her simple affairs — first as a dutiful son but later with power of attorney.

And so the final chapter. A board went up bearing the name of a Leeds based Estate Agent.

For Sale, with 3/4 acre,
freehold barn conversion in
need of considerable modernisation.
Planning permission obtained.

A snip at £175,000. These were the 1980s when anything with four walls and even half a roof hardly ever needed publication. Newsteads was taken before any of the local papers (the Huddersfield Examiner; the Halifax Courier; even the Brighouse Echo) ever reached street level.

Nigel arranged everything, not losing sight of the fact that the interest on £175,000 would just about cover the cost of the residential home he had selected for his mother. He was reassuring.

"It's all for the best, mother."

Mother, still numbed from the bereavement, acquiesced by nods and inarticulate murmurings.

"The land will be sold." Nod.

"The stone from the outbuildings will be sold off". Nod. "And the furniture — such as it is — will be taken care of". Nod.

"The home we've arranged for you is lovely and new. And you won't have a penny to pay. We can visit you there once a month at least."

For the first time Maria spoke. "I'll not be lonely. Sam and me's been on our own a bit now. We've framed afore: we'll frame again."

Nigel looked at his mother with an enigmatic expression. "Whatever made you think that Sam would be admitted? This is a residential home, standards of hygiene must be maintained. Sam would never be allowed. After all he is a farm dog."

"I'm not going then. I'd rather stay here. Newstead is my home." The indomitable pose was held with difficulty.

"Mother, you can't stay here. Newsteads isn't yours any longer."

What further pressure was applied I can't honestly say. But I was there, by chance, when a car arrived to take Maria off in one direction and a Land Rover which took Sam off in another. The looks that they gave each other as the vehicles pulled away are best left unrecorded.

* * *

There is a footnote to this tale. Newsteads was sold and a refurbishment was planned. However, before any long term settlement could be made, a compulsory purchase order was implemented and Newsteads disappeared under the waters of a reservoir.

Sounds in the Night

"I don't know how you stand it out here: it's much too quiet for me".

I'd never considered the matter until friends stopped overnight on a holiday trip to Scotland. It had been an ordinary kind of night and my question at breakfast (Did you sleep well?) was more of a conversational gambit than a serious enquiry.

It was the kind of morning that made me glad that we lived where we did; in one of a cluster of cottages and farms protected from the north by the comfortable foothills of Ingleborough, but high enough to look out and across the fell side with its enduring dry stone walls and, here and there, a traditional North country barn.

A mist covered the village down hill from us: a heat haze that we knew would burn off before mid morning.

"How can a place be too quiet?" I pondered this question and then put it to my wife. That didn't help.

"It all depends on what you mean by quiet", she said. "By their standards, it must be quietish". Our friends lived just south of Sheffield close to the M1.

I thought about this; then: "I've a good mind to put it to the test. I'll stay up 'til after midnight and then go out and test how quiet it is."

118

By means of raised eyebrows my wife managed silently to cast doubts upon my ability to stay awake after midnight.

It really was a beautiful night. The moon was almost full and the cloudless sky did have that texture and colour of velvet so beloved of romantic novelists. The hills stood out sharply against the sky. The valley sparkled with isolated house lights. There was a definite but momentary chill in the air and a hint of mist above the village. It was actually quite mild when I got used to it. Everywhere visually beautiful but, apparently, utterly quiet. I moved away from the corner of the house, down the lane towards the road. I waited. I may have dozed, leaning against the wall; it wouldn't have been the first time.

Gradually I became aware of noises all around me. Not loud noises; often only whispered sounds or, perhaps, vibrations absorbed through my feet and not my ears. There were rustles of small mammals sneaking through the grass; the hens in their shed were restless and clattered and clucked around. The eerie clicks and screeches of a tawny owl in the ash tree at the end of the lane contrasted with the conventional too-wit-to-woo of the barn owl from its nest in the barn.

Then, like an orchestra tuning up an instrument at a time, other animal sounds joined in. The sharp bark of a dog fox close by under the scarr was answered by the unearthly shriek of a vixen far away across the valley. I hope that it meant a great deal more to the dog fox than it did to me. I shivered with imagination rather than real fear. I did, however certainly hear the insistent thump of rabbits telling each other to watch out, then taking evasive action underground.

As I turned for home, fully justified in my assertion that the countryside is not a quiet place, I heard it. A long, drawn out, quavering wail. It seemed to go on and on; up and down the scale in quarter tones. The warm air became suddenly chilly. Feeling a curious need of human company I went indoors and invited my wife to listen also. She is a musician and might just have an explanation — that was my excuse at least. We waited; nothing. Everything else that had been noisy five minutes earlier was, seemingly, stupefied into silence as I was.

Then, once more, that extended banshee wail. I thought of wolves and, irrationally, of witches' cats on the prowl. I was aware quite suddenly of my wife's almost silent laughter.

"That's Arabella, you idiot."

"Arabella?"

"Yes. Kath Metcalfe's Afghan hound."

And anti-climactically that is exactly what it was. That was the first time (but not the last, since we later owned one) that I heard an Afghan hound in full song.

Under an almost full moon on a clear night it is, shall we say, an invigorating sound.

Heading North

Just north of Leeds on the A1 road there is the most heartening roadsign that I know. I have approached it hundreds of times and each time the same glow of expectancy lights up my mind. It says:

WETHERBY AND THE NORTH.

The root cause of my delight is many-fold. Two reasons, however, rise above the rest: Wetherby is many miles north of the England/Yorkshire boundary and "The North" is still further on; and Wetherby itself is the National Hunt racecourse that many regard as "the Cheltenham of the North".

It is a well known fact that I am enthusiastic about National Hunt racing. Flat racing leaves me cold but watching superb horses, being ridden at speed in competition, over fences and hurdles is stimulating to mind and body alike. And it must be made clear that it is the sport itself, not the betting upon the outcome, that really counts. Gambling upon horses in any case is seriously flawed as a means of making money and also in its entertainment value. If one loses, the money is gone and the intrinsic merits of the race, the joy that comes from watching horses in action, is gone too. On the other hand, if one wins, the immediate reaction is;

"Why didn't I put more on and really clean up?" Definitely a no win situation.

In addition to Wetherby, the North has many racecourses. They range from the gloriously eccentric on the one hand to the well appointed (like Wetherby itself and Haydock Park) on the other. In a class of its own is Aintree. Most endearing is the rarely used but highly regarded racecourse at Cartmel. It opens for two Bank Holiday meetings a year and that is all. Its charm lies in a combination of three factors: (1) visitors view the racing from inside the circular track and not alongside it; (2) the course runs, for quite some distance, along the garden bottoms of a row of houses and (3) the last couple of furlongs before the run-in pass through a wood so that no spectator can see the action! The very stuff of country life and accepted as normal by the many hundreds who attend and are accustomed to the makeshift courses sometimes erected for team chases or hunter trials.

Another course memorable for more than just racing is Hexham. Hexham is set high up in the remote lands of the north within walking distance of Hadrian's wall. This is the course where it snows uphill and where jockeys can legitimately claim that they were blown off course down the back straight, and use the excuse as a plea at a stewards' enquiry into unexpectedly poor performance.

To return to Wetherby. In addition to its National Hunt Calendar, Wetherby offers its facilities to many local hunts as the venue for their annual point-to-point meetings. The Badsworth, the Rockwood Harriers and the Sinnington hunts are three which come to mind.

Point-to-points and hunter trials along with team chases, sheep dog trialing and game fairs, are all glorious opportunities for people with similar interests to enjoy a day out; to eat and drink together and to take up a topic of conversation that was broken off last year. Social distinctions are set aside and the only people who attract suspicion are those who wear brand new Barbours! They are likely to be either poseurs or hunting abolitionists trying to blend in, in order to pick up valuable intelligence.

It often happens that point-to-points and similar activities will produce genuinely top class horses. Trainers local to Wetherby and Malton and Pickering (and there are many) will often enter horses that have racing potential, or superannuated champions who no longer race at the highest level, but are regularly hunted; which is the main criterion for entry. So it was that my own personal equine hero, after honourable retirement, could be seen running against horses that one saw daily at livery or with the local hunts. His name was Night Nurse.

I could write a book about Night Nurse. Perhaps I shall, one day. He was trained by Peter Easterby near Malton. In his early years Night Nurse won two Champion Hurdles at Cheltenham in the mid-70s and most other hurdling trophies as well. This in itself was a considerable achievement: it was much more so when one considers that racing at the same time there were no fewer than five other hurdlers who were Champion

Hurdle quality. Amongst them were the legendary Sea Pigeon and Monksfield.

The tales I could tell! But there is space for only one. The Templegate Hurdle at Aintree in 1977. Both horses were champion hurdlers of previous years and Night Nurse was the reigning champion, having slogged through the Cheltenham mud a little over a fortnight earlier to beat his great rival Monksfield, by two lengths. Now, on April 2nd, conditions and circumstances were very different. It was a hot day and the going was firm underfoot.

There were eight other horses in the race but everyone accepted that it was really a duel. Night Nurse, the older by one year, was a big, powerful animal with a style of jumping which suggested that he was not jumping at all; simply flying low. He later went into steeplechasing over fences and there again he triumphed, reaching the very highest, Gold Cup, ranking; although the nearest he ever came to the trophy was second. By contrast Monksfield was a small, compact Irish stallion with a beautiful head, a curious leg action and, allegedly, a great sense of humour. To see him before a race was to see an animal full of himself and loving every moment. By contrast, Night Nurse at home or in the parade ring always looked dejected: as if he could hardly walk a mile let alone run three at something like 30 miles an hour. It was all an act of course, an equine con trick to fool the opposition. Maybe so, but he was supposed to have a defective heart valve and been "written off" years earlier.

Right from the start of the race the plan was clear. The Monksfield camp determined to harry the champion and not let him get away with anything. And so it went on right round the course. The play paid off. Night Nurse was forced into a number of jumping errors from which only a horse of his quality, and a jockey of Paddy Broderick's experience and skill, could have hoped to recover.

Three flights of hurdles from home (15 lengths ahead of their nearest opponent) they were locked together: literally head to head. And so it remained for what seemed an endless run in. First one horse would draw ahead. The other would rally and the order changed. Again . . . and again . . . and again . . .

They crossed the line together. Horses and jockeys alike were exhausted. And then the wait began. Photographs were consulted, murmurings were heard as to whether they actually touched and hindered between hurdles. When the result finally came Aintree exploded with emotion and relief. A dead heat: official acknowledgement. It was what everyone knew in their hearts the result should be. You would expect that such a momentous event would go down in sporting folk lore and be recounted over and over again. It would have been but for one important happening.

Less than an hour later, Red Rum won the Grand National for a record third time.

"On Your Bike" — As the Saying Goes

I am not an habitual law-breaker and generally speaking the ten commandments are safe in my hands. However, like every one else I have occasional lapses.

On this occasion it was trivial and harmless in itself but strangely enough the sense of guilt was out of all proportion.

As was so often the case over a period of about 10 years, we were moving house. This time it was a serious move which needed a combination of the logistical skills and the talents of Napoleon and Hannibal. In a word, my wife.

After a twenty five year teaching stint in the same school, she felt an overwhelming urge to uproot and remove. I had a contract that was binding for a further term. She ended in July — with ceremonial and festivity appropriate to one who had dedicated the prime of her life to one job. I had to teach on until December.

In consequence, we spent the summer holiday moving house and getting her settled in. In early September I returned to the bleak upland between

126

Huddersfield and Rochdale to spend three months in a caravan with "all mod cons". This meant a heavy duty electricity cable from the utility room of our friends' house (whose paddock we were using) along with a key that admitted me to a room with a washbasin and loo.

What more could a grass-widower ask for, or expect? I even had my own transport — a Honda 90 two stroke motor bike — borrowed from our son who had moved on to more illustrious things. I am hopelessly unmechanical but I loved that bike. I treasured my first provisional licence and made a point of polishing the machine, including the L-plates every week.

My first major adventure was getting the Honda up from Essex — where our son lived — via Warwickshire, where our daughters lived — to Pennine Yorkshire. My wife, who loves driving and dreams, even now, of owning an Aston Martin, planned me a route. I was to take the rustic route and arrange to meet her at selected points where motorways and rustic routes came together.

The circumstances of that journey would fill a volume the size of this one. We broke our journey in the Midlands and then went on; me at my mechanical snail's pace, my wife at a more practical speed, from her point of view at least.

What was left of the summer holiday passed quickly. For three months apart from an occasional weekend together, we went our separate ways. For me the setting and the views were superb in every direction. Although man-made, the sinuous Scammonden Dam and reservoir were highly appropriate and somehow, that view from the caravan across the road and across the waters will always be amongst my dearest Pennine scenes. I quickly settled in.

I also quickly became, not bored, but restless. I had work to do, I had reading and writing to keep up with. I love solitude — usually. A nightly phone call to my wife, requiring a walk of about a mile and a half helped. And in spite of being able to do something like 125 miles to the gallon I felt that the exercise did me good.

As always, she had the solution. "Advertise coaching or tuition at home, in the local shops and Post Offices. I pointed out that I was without a telephone and, effectively, of no fixed address. She became impatient and I fed in another couple of coins. "Then ask around at school. Someone's bound to want a bit of a push in basic Maths and English!" And they did of course.

I soon had a clientele in the Huddersfield area whom I could reach by motorbike: Elland, Honley, Kirkburton and one or two more. The pupils were all about 12 years old and candidates for Common Entrance.

It worked very well. I met people, I enjoyed riding the bike and, in addition, I was paid well for my efforts. Having lived in the Pennines for over a quarter of a century I soon got used to the weather, although I never actually got to enjoy having sleet driven into my face at 40 miles an hour (the sleet, not the bike; I never topped 40 except with a following wind).

Which brings me full circle to my opening sentence about breaking the law. It was quite simple really. I had been visiting Elland and I was travelling across town to

Kirkburton. The weather was vile and my mind must have gone into a self-locking mode. As I crossed Holywell Green I suddenly found myself going up the slip-road onto the M62. Remember I had only a 90cc bike and two very conspicuous L-plates at the time. On the principle of "in for a penny, in for a pound", I rode at modest speed close to the edge of the hard shoulder. I kept everything figuratively crossed and imagined what a friend of mine — he worked on the Halifax Courier I remember — might do if I got caught.

I couldn't get off until Brighouse by which time I was late for my lesson and had twice as far still to travel. I stopped to ring my apology. It was then that I was overcome by helpless, nervous, laughter. As I dialled the number, I suddenly remembered that the pupil I was about to visit at his home, was the son of an Assistant Chief Constable of the West Yorkshire Police.

Voluntary Overtime

Imagine, if you will, four dogs. One, an Irish Setter in the prime of life, two, his more austere, but equally idiosyncratic "cousin" a Gordon Setter — just out of puppyhood; and two Jack Russells — mother and daughter — simply being Jack Russells.

This was the extempore pack that roamed the farm whilst we, the six of us, slaved away at getting the hay bales into a Dutch barn before it started raining — again.

Let me explain. The setter was the Mighty Mungo, who appears again and again in my reminiscences because he was unique (to me, at least) and also because he lived to an incredible age; by setter standards that is.

The two Jack Russells belonged to the farm. And I cannot imagine any farm, especially one that doubles as a livery stable, that does not have at least one of these extraordinary, exhilarating and often infuriating little dogs.

The Gordon Setter was the property of a grandson of the farmer and his wife who lived on a farm high up by Emley Moor mast.

Together these dogs would go up and hunt moles, hedgehogs and the farm cats. And such was their collective prowess that all they managed to catch was fleas from the hedgehogs and a series of scratched noses from the cats, who were more than a match for any kind of hound.

When they tired of this they would chase around the paddock (always in a clockwise direction) an evil minded mare called Sorcery, a Cleveland Bay X thoroughbred who has her own slot elsewhere. On an undisclosed signal every one of the animals reversed and she, Sorcery, chased them instead: anti-clockwise, of course.

Whilst all this was going on, the humans got on with the job of humping haybales on to a low loading trailer attached to a tractor of extreme antiquity. When the load was made up it was driven (often by my wife) and backed carefully into a barn with no more than inches to spare either side.

The first time we helped out Arthur, the farmer, well advanced into his 70s, drove the tractor. That is until he saw my wife struggling with one of the bales; the weight of which caught at her already evident arthritis. It was particularly noticeable by contrast with his own daughter and wife, both of whom, with no apparent difficulty, could pick up a bale in each hand and with no struggle at all position them both unerringly on the trailer. He got off the tractor seat and said:

"Coom on, lass, I'll tack over there; you drive yon tractor."

He was tactful enough not to add "If you can". My wife has always been an ardent driver who could tow, and back, a caravan into just about any space. But whatever he thought at first, Arthur never had any cause for complaint about her driving. Even though she had never handled a tractor before.

The tractor itself must have outstripped all of us in age, having metal spoked wheels and possessing the curious habit of being started on petrol before switching over to paraffin when warmed up. In this respect it was just a giant primus stove on wheels.

When daylight eventually went (or it started to rain again) we packed up and all the hay timers; farmer, wife, daughter, grandson and the two of us crowded into the farm kitchen where the housewife had provided supper. And as for the dogs, they eventually returned scratched, flea-ridden and totally filthy. We were all tired, but all of us (dogs and humans alike) always lived to fight another day.

There's Always a
Name For It

It would be a brave man (or a foolish one) who would say out loud "The best bit of the Pennines is . . ." Brave or foolish is open to question, but he certainly wouldn't be a Dalesman — a true Dalesman that is.

Despite the bewildering variations of landscape; the diversity of rock formations; the patchwork of densely industrial centres and the seemingly limitless vistas of treeless moors or peat hags; the Pennines are an entity. They are an organic whole from Edale in Derbyshire, midway between Manchester and Sheffield; up to the Scottish borders and even beyond. This chain of countryside is "all of a piece". To try and claim which are "the best bits" is like comparing one's foot with one's hand or a canine tooth with a molar.

One's favourite bits? Well, that's another matter altogether. My wife enjoys most those gaunt and treeless gritstone moors; the peat hags; the bilberry fellsides and the cotton grass bogs. I prefer the light, bright limestone with its clints and grikes, its pavement and its scarrs, its sinkholes and the sudden appearance, almost at one's feet, of a bubbling stream of pure, clear water. The stream that bubbles out from the foot of Malham Cove, immortalised by Charles Kingsley's *Water Babies*, looks unimpressive enough. It has been proved, by using dyestuffs, that it last saw the light of day disappearing down a sink hole high above on the top of the cove. Unimpressive it may look but it is the start of the River Aire nevertheless.

Jointly, our favourite bits centre upon the Three Peaks area. We have variety enough to satisfy both our preferences and more besides. Just as there is variation in members of a family so there is variety in members of the Pennine heights. But there is a family resemblance which is due to the underlying patterns of the rocks.

At a certain point on the return road from Morecambe to Lancaster, all Three Peaks can be seen together. Because I have a romantic imagination I am reminded of a breeding ewe (Whernside) and two lambs nearby (Ingleborough and Pen-y-ghent). The angle changes and there, round to the right, is another lamb, a triplet who has somehow become separated from the flock. Pendle Hill.

Books have been written about Pendle Hill. Topographical books, geology books, romantic books about the witches of Pendle; and accounts have been included in his memoirs by no less a fellwanderer than A. Wainwright himself. And that alone must confer a kind of immortality.

I must be honest and say that I have never climbed Pendle. I have only seen it from afar. Now, when age is no longer kind to me, I may never be prevailed upon. I am content to see it at a distance: standing proud and solitary, looking much higher than its actual height. The view from the top on a clear day must be terrific.

But despite my reservations I welcome Pendle Hill into my intimate family of special places. Why? Because of its name. To an etymologist and word lover the name is a gem. It demonstrates exactly why language is so fascinating. A German philosopher, Von Sebelling, once described architecture as frozen music. To me place names are frozen history. Centuries of history are packed into the simple name Pendle Hill.

"Pen" is a fairly well known Celtic word for a hill summit — it crops up everywhere

"Hyll" is the Saxon word for hill which is only slightly different from the modern-day hill.

Pendle Hill, therefore, is "hill-hill-hill". This very assertive affirmation takes us a long way towards an appreciation of the feelings our Pennine ancestors had for Pendle, and Pen-y-ghent also, down the ages.

Come to that, what about the Pennines themselves? PENnines: a range of hills with distinguishing separate peaks. A nice try, a plausible derivation. It could be; except for the fact that the earliest definite use of the name appears in the 18th century. The 18th century was when the Grand Tour of Europe was a necessary stage in the education of English gentlemen. Out there in Europe are the Appennine Mountains. Suppose, just suppose, the returning son of a wealthy Yorkshire mill-owner appropriated the name to impress friends and family and to put Yorkshire where it rightfully belongs. Not the hub of the universe certainly: but the backbone of Europe without a doubt.

135

Thoughts on the Pennine Way

To walk even a part of the Pennine Way — and I have only ever done it in part — always reminds me of Tolkien's *Lord of the Rings*. When Frodo and his companions set out on their mystical journey, he chants a rhyme:-

> "The Road goes ever on and on
> Down from the door where it began.
> Now far ahead the Road has gone,
> And I must follow if I can . . ."

There are plenty of books about the Pennine Way; practical, historical, even romantic. Books to suit all tastes. This brief piece will add nothing to what has gone before. To be truthful, it is not about the Pennine Way at all. It is about my responses to it from standpoints where my wanderings and its clearly defined route coincide.

Black and White, Dark and Light: call them what you will. The truth is that a substantial length of the Pennine Way can be divided into these contrasted regions by completing the equations white equals limestone and black equals millstone grit. Both types of landscape have their adherents, and partisans who can (indeed do) waste hours of valuable time arguing to and fro. However, both parties can see virtue in the other's point of view. That tolerance is what makes the Pennine Way a unity, a genuine long distance footpath and not just a cobbling together of separate fragments of trackway.

Looking back at Tolkien's rhyme; whose was the door from which the adventure began? Curiously enough in the case of the Pennine Way, it was the door of the *Daily Herald* newspaper. The *Herald* had an *Afoot in Britain* feature. It was written by Tom Stephenson. For forty years Tom Stephenson had lived in Pennine Lancashire. His life had been uneventful and during periods of unemployment Tom wandered and roamed the Pennine country which he loved. He pioneered the Ramblers' Association and in 1933 he joined the Herald with a vast itinerary of routes at his command and very strong views about right of access and "the right to roam". This freedom of access philosophy endeared him to the left wing politics of the *Daily Herald* and his journalistic career took off.

In 1935 two adventurous American girls wrote to Tom asking for advice on how to walk the spine of Britain. The idea fired-up Tom Stephenson's imagination and, feeding off his own Pennine wanderings, the Pennine Way took shape.

Tom was unequivocally a "dark" man: a lover of millstone grit. And so is my wife who likes nothing better than to climb the Pennines and gaze across miles of undulating peat bog and high moor with its nardus grass, its bilberry and the white tufts of cotton grass in the really boggy spots.

Drive with us out of Holmfirth by one of two trans-Pennine routes. The one, via Holme Moss, runs vaguely south west and joins up with the road to Hyde or Stalybridge. The other, more northerly route, runs westward to Greenfield and Oldham. Both traverse upland areas memorably called Black Hill and Featherbed Moss. The northerly route — which actually crosses the Pennine Way at one point — crosses Saddleworth Moor, which has its natural bleakness and inhospitable terrain made more chilling by memories of Brady and Hindley.

This time we didn't drive that far, but only as far as the Pennine Way. We walk a short distance — just far enough to lose the car. We look; we listen. The view is of some blue green desert with bright green patches of sphagnum moss warning the visitor to stay clear. The Pennine answer to quicksand. We dutifully obey. The sky is immense, a huge canopy unequalled anywhere except in the Fens. The cloud seems tangible. We watch a rainstorm building in the south west and watch it race towards us, borne on a wind that anywhere else would be called a gale but up here is accorded the dignity of "a fairish blow". Retreat to the car is the only sensible thing to do and we go back by a different road — a very minor road — to the relative comforts of Meltham. We pass one of the manufacturing greats of the area: David Brown, builder of tractors and the engine for the renowned Aston Martin car. And then home.

Meltham was reached in no time at all. Had we gone in opposite direction we would just as easily have reached Greater Manchester. Yet up on the top there was neither sight nor sound of either conurbation. Uncanny and almost unreal: the Black Hill area is timeless and totally remote. How ironic that the only visible vertical should be Holme Moss television mast: symbol of communications and intimacy across the land.

That other great symbol of trans-Pennine communications, the M62, has its own part to play in our story. Not far from Junction 22 there is a beautiful sweeping bridge that spans the motorway. It stands as a bold symbol for humanity over materialism: the Pennine Way bridge.

The planning and ratifying of the building of the M62 aroused opposition and anger in the walking fraternity. The motorway would cut in two the Pennine Way. The uninterrupted trail of 270 miles, for which many had worked and accomplished would be lost.

On this occasion red tape and political dithering did not prevail. The cause was taken up by Sir Ernest Marples — one time minister of the crown — whose passion and energy for the cause of walkers saw the project through. That bridge is his memorial.

* * *

At no time can I remember being persuaded to visit Malham, Cove and Tarn, between April and November.

The closest parallel I can think of for Malham district at Bank Holidays is the ambience of a huge shopping mall (Metro Centre; Merry Hill; Lakeside or Bluewater) at the run-up to Christmas.

When we lived, as we did for such a long time, less than eight miles as the crow flies from the Malham area, we hardly visited Malham at all. If visiting family and friends wanted to see, for example, where Charles Kingsley located the *Water Babies*, we made a cautious foray by the back road at Stainforth and drove across the moor to Arncliffe. And even then we would take the scenic route via Halton Gill in the hope that the unparalleled view of Pen-y-ghent might stop them in their tracks. After all, the Pennine Way does go over the top of it.

However, since we are celebrating the Pennine Way in its entirety, we have a duty to visit Malham Moor. It was here, 30 years after Tom Stephenson first mapped out a route for two young Americans, that the Way was made official and opened with splendour and ceremony. On the 24th April 1965 Tom Stephenson himself addressed the crowds of walkers and climbers after the Minister of Land and Resources, the Rt Hon F Wiley "topped out" the venture so to speak.

The black and white world of Charles Kingsley's Water Babies is a far cry from the topsy-turvydom of Lewis Carroll. And yet there is a tenuous link between the Looking Glass world and the Craven district which contains Malham. The link is geological. Look at Pen-y-ghent, at Ingleborough and you will see the rock sequence that gives the unique shape or pattern to the landscape. This is, going upwards, limestone, millstone grit and a topping of narrow bands or strata of different kinds of rocks — the Yordale series. It is their different resistances to weathering that creates the step-like profiles of the Three Peaks and elsewhere.

Returning home from Malham we would often take the main road up through Settle, along the old road to Clapham and thence to Ingleton and beyond. This took us up over Buckhaw Brow; steep and impressive. Here we are in topsy turvy land. Towering high to the right-hand are cliffs of limestone, light, bright and clad in the vivid green of pasture grass. Away to the left the "black" landscape of typical millstone grit, very many feet below.

Who turned the landscape upside down and put the gritstone lower than the limestone? Answer, the forces of nature. Buckhaw Brow follows the line of the south Craven Fault — one of a pair of fault lines of the kind that created the great rift valley of East Africa.

Unimaginable years ago the earth moved; it didn't rotate but great portions slipped and sheared; rose and bulged until the rocks appeared to lie in the wrong sequence.

Even after many years I still didn't quite get used to it. Fortunately the fault had missed altogether the place where we lived.

* * *

"It is during the night of 14th / 15th January and the year is 1968. Here, on the top of Great Dun Fell, some two miles south east of Cross Fell the wind speed has just been recorded at 134 miles per hour." Unfortunately this is not a transcript from my diary. I wasn't there to experience the record speed for England and Wales. It was someone else who braved the elements and I am simply quoting.

The account does, however, show just how one can be "climatically challenged" at a height of less than 3000 feet. And on the route of the Pennine Way too.

I have seen the landscape of Strathnaver — in Sutherland — under curtains of rain. I have travelled by night across Rannoch Moor in winter with the moon exaggerating every trough and crest of drifted snow. But neither can outrank Cross Fell in winter.

Because the top is a rounded plateau and not a peak or a ridge like Striding Edge, one loses the sense of altitude. Pen-y-ghent, some 600 feet less high gives the impression of being a mountain because it rises sheer from a relatively gentle landscape. The same is true of Pendle Hill.

Cross Fell simply bulges up from a landscape already bulging at above 2,000 feet and so its altitude in real terms is not noticed.

The same of course is true upon a much grander scale with Ben Nevis — which rises sheer from sea level to over 4000 feet — and the Cairngorms, which have a common altitude above 3000 feet, with a few peaks topping 4000, but scarcely recognised as mountains at all.

For all its non-dramatic appearance from a distance, Cross Fell, along with its companions, Great Dun Fell and Knock Fell, is a force to be reckoned with: a serious warning in some walkers' manuals: " . . difficult and stern terrain rightly the preserve of the experienced." And A. Wainwright himself once called Cross Fell "monarch of the Pennines".

Amongst genuine climbers and walkers there is humility: a willingness to proclaim abysmal failures as freely as great achievements. And everyone will have a collection of both to pass on either as triumphs or cautionary tales. I do not put myself into that exalted category. I simply love walking the Pennines and, maybe, scrambling a bit at need. I do, however, have a cautionary tale to offer.

It was a typical high Pennine day; misty with scudding cloud and intermittent rain. We were resting before trekking southwards to Great Dun Fell and then down to Dufton. From there, getting home by car was an easy option. The hard bit was behind us; a two-day trek from Alston.

When we arrived on the summit of Cross Fell there came one of those inexplicable windows in the weather. To the north the Cheviots glistened like the broad back of a giant whale. To the south the peaks of Pennine Yorkshire stood proud and clearly defined. Then the day closed in once more.

We huddled together, drank coffee and nibbled Kendal mint cake. We felt almost reluctant to stir. There was no wind and the mist sat upon the landscape and depressed it.

I heard a cough and a clattering of loose rocks. Coming towards us through the mist was a figure; a most unusual figure to meet on the top of the highest summit in Pennine Yorkshire. As he came closer we saw a man in a deerstalker hat, a heavy tweed overcoat, plus-two trousers and the kind of boots that miners wear — or workers on building sites; heavy, black and fitted with protective steel toecaps. He carried an old fashioned knapsack that was obviously an ex-army side pack.

As if this was not enough to shatter our composure, he was talking out loud, not to himself but to his companion: a small, bedraggled dachshund. We did not have time to introduce ourselves: he made the first move.

"Are we on t' top?"

"Aye."

"Then weer's t'pub?"

"What pub?"

"Aye, t'pub." He waved a sodden book. "Yon says theer's a pub hereabouts. The 'ighest in England."

His book was Wainwright's classic "Pennine Way Companion."

Grins were masked and chuckles stifled. But how can you tell a middle-aged man (complete with dachshund) that his present location is not Tan Hill, as he clearly expected, but Cross Fell, some 16 treacherous miles north west of where he expected to be?

As gently as I could I explained the situation. We suggested that he came down to Dufton with us and then made his way to somewhere like Appleby and thence to wherever he hoped to spend the night.

He brooded a bit, took out a thermos from his knapsack and refreshed himself. Then:

"Nay, lad, you'd best knock on. We take it steady, 'im and me." And the dog snuggled up to his legs.

Reluctantly we left them to their rest. At Appleby we rang the fell rescue and put them wise. Our natural concern was greeted with laughter.

"You've met old Albert then. He's allus doin' it — gettin' lost like. But 'e's 'armless enough. If ever 'e gets lost, 'e clips little dog onto a long lead and says "Coom lad, let's be off 'ome". It works every time."

I do not know to this day who was trying to wind me up. Was it Albert or the leader of the fell rescue? Perhaps I'll never know — but I'll keep asking whenever I'm in the area.

Pennine Poetry

Many books have been written about the Pennines. Some are strictly topographical and deal exclusively with landscape, climate and vegetation: all very accurate but mostly deadly dull. But if anyone asks me to "show them the Pennines as they really are" I produce a page of some 24 lines of poetry and say, "There you are; it's all there. Just read it!"

The poem *Wind* is one of a number of poems by the late Ted Hughes which encapsulate the very essence of that unique landscape. With the possible exception of Emily Brontë nobody else ever came anywhere near. Sylvia Plath, when she was married to Ted Hughes, tried hard and *Hardcastle Crags* is very good. But Plath was always more concerned with the effect of places (and things) on her own emotions. She was unable to display, with intense and dispassionate words, the actual place, as it exists, and would continue to exist even if you had never heard about it or written about it. Ted Hughes did just that, not only with *Wind* but with *Pennines in April* also and less obviously in many another poem or story.

Like Ted Hughes, I, too, have experienced ". . . the brunt wind that dented the balls of my eyes. The tent

146

of the hills drummed and strained its guyrope". That is exactly how it feels; the very senses are hammered into an uncomfortable shape. I have tried long and often to describe the intensity of wind as an experience. Nothing I have ever written can compare with the precision and economy of "The wind flung a magpie away and a black-backed gull bent like an iron bar slowly . . ."

Less in her actual poems but constantly in *Wuthering Heights* Emily Brontë gets it right. Even just thinking about it as I am now takes me back to Grey Scarrs, a cottage that we lived in in the shade of Pen-y-ghent. The building was long and low and built from local limestone. The walls were at least four feet thick (if the depth of the window sills was anything to go by). I remember once being in bed with tonsillitis — a rare event in my usually healthy life. It was winter, snow covered the fells and the fields. The trees were black scribbles against the grey sky. I lay there and read *Wuthering Heights* until I was uncertain whether the storm that raged was real or induced by the intensity of the writing.

A banging brought me to my senses: I was just about to look to the window and let in the importunate Cathy when my wife, from the doorway, broke the spell. "How you can just lie there without the light on and wide awake I just don't know. It's four o'clock. I've brought you some lemon tea and a sandwich. We'll eat properly when I get back." At the time she taught music at Giggleswick School and did an evening session in lieu of a daytime one.

That cottage, in many respects holds some of my fondest memories. Both in itself and its location it was as near perfect as one can get. We were young and (fairly) newly married and we shared together a landscape and a lifestyle that we both enjoyed and still love after all these years.

Whether the location is specified or not, many of these reminiscences are centred there or thereabouts.

Height of Perfection

Although it is less than 750 feet high, Hampsfell, near Grange, creates a disproportionate sense of altitude when the surrounding landscape is viewed from the Hospice near the top.

We climbed it early by a track through Eggerslack Wood. Already, with the sun barely up, we could sense the potential hotness of the day. The air was heavy with pollen, scented by woodland flowers, humid with the rising early mist and vigorous with the vibrations of myriad insects.

We emerged through a grove where last year's bracken lay bronzed and crisp, the new shoots already growing slender and tall, coiled like tiny shepherds' crooks before opening. They are beautiful and delicate but curiously tenacious, and anathema to farmers and shepherds.

A scramble over rock strewn pasture brought us to the top: to a bare limestone plateau eroded and carved into a pavement of huge slabs. The turf between was undulating and dotted with anthills. Solitary hawthorns and wind-bent silver birches grow there with their roots deep in the clefts and fissures of the rock.

The contrast with the wood we had recently climbed through is most striking and curiously moving. The plateau is silent except for a trilling skylark invisible above and the plaintive crying of curlews, which have the effect of making the solitude more intense. I stumbled on the uneven ground and startled a shelduck, black and white and goose-like in form, which flew up no more than fifteen feet away and struck off in the direction of the sea.

From the Hospice itself — a commemorative structure about 200 years old and built on the site of an ancient and no longer extant building — the view is astounding. The northern skyline is dominated by the peaks of Central Lakeland: Scafell, Great Gable, Coniston Old Man, the Langdales. Further round there is the familiar profile of Ingleborough twenty miles away. Incredibly remote, the Snowdon Massif of North Wales is visible through binoculars to the South.

The sun rose higher and as we watched a heat haze obscured those features one by one, closing in and leaving, in the end, a circumscribed perimeter with the Cartmell Valley, rich and wooded on one side and the heavily green expanses of the flat salt marshes down beyond the woods on the other. Beyond are the tidal flats of Morecambe Bay. It is here that the sense of exaggerated height is greatest.

Hampsfell: remote and beautiful but accessible to all who are willing to climb the relatively gentle slope which offers en route variety and satisfaction at every turn.

A last look before descending and my eyes lingered on Humphrey Head, which was to be the second leg of

ION

the walk. This feature has been likened to a whale stranded on the foreshore. Seen from Flookburgh, across the marshes and the disused airfield, the comparison is apt. It is a massive limestone block jutting out in craggy isolation from the north shore of Morecambe Bay. At the foot of the crag at the western side there is a holy well, the waters from which are said to have curative powers of a potent kind. Bottles of this water were once sold at Grange and else- where around the coast.

There are also many interesting and unusual plants nearby, including deadly nightshade. This was once cultivated by the monks of Furness Abbey and they extracted from it the powerful alkaloid belladonna, which they used in certain cases of heart failure. The very name, Belladonna, is a reminder also of the mediaeval use of the plant in cosmetic preparations.

Leaving the well we walked up onto the top and were impressed by the crispness of the limestone turf. It was cropped short by sheep and spread out to where the woods begin and cascade down from the top to overrun the sheltered side. Gorse bushes abound, smelling spicy and proving irresistible to insects, including the bees from a small huddle of hives nearby. Closer contact with the limestone turf reveals hummocks that make walking hazardous for one whose eyes are everywhere but downcast. These hummocks are anthills — thousands of them — each one a colony of tiny yellow ants, forever scurrying to repair the damage done by unwary booted feet. Once I surprised a green woodpecker planted foursquare on his splayed

151

feet probing and eating both ants and grubs with impartial delight. He was so preoccupied that I was able to approach within a few feet before he took fright and fled.

The devastation was enormous. The anthill was torn apart: ants scurried about carrying eggs and fragments of soil in a frantic attempt to put their house in order. But they worked in vain. Attracted by I know not what stimulus the enemy arrived.

More ants: robbers, huge, black and predatory. Like a human army bent on plundering and ravaging their way to victory the invading ants overcame the defenders and carried off their booty: ant eggs, grubs and even mature ants of the smaller, weaker kind.

It made me wonder at the vast and complex web of nature where the law that is basic runs, kill or be killed: put another way, Survival of the Fittest. This was brought home to me even more forcibly a little later when I came across the carcase of a green woodpecker being picked over by a carrion crow.

Before returning for tea I looked back across the route I had been travelling since early morning. From this viewpoint it looked like a landscape in miniature and the harmony between "wild" nature and the settlements of Man seemed ideal: the most natural thing in the world.

A Pram up Pen-y-Ghent

Buddhists, so I'm told, have a system of worship which is also a means of getting rid of stress. It is called a mantra. It is a word (or sound) which is repeated over and over again as an aid to meditation. If I were a Buddhist, my mantra would be "Pen-y-ghent . . . Pen-y-ghent . . Pen-y-ghent."

The very sound of the word is soothing. Whispered over and over again it obliges in dentists' waiting rooms no less than off-setting road rage in traffic jams.

In "real life" it is one of the three peaks. Those magnificent weathered blocks of limestone surmounted by millstone grit and a diversity of layers of shale and sandstone and much else. These three, Pen-y-ghent, Ingleborough and Whernside dominate the landscape and are visible on a clear day from Queensbury, near Bradford, to the South-East and from the road between Morecambe and Lancaster to the West. All are impressive (and so are many other lesser fells) but only Pen-y-ghent is beautiful — from all angles.

As mountains go, it isn't big (something under 3,000 feet) but it is in the same league as Mount Kilimanjaro in Tanzania which is nearly 20,000 feet. And whereas Kilimanjaro had Ernest Hemingway to extol it, Pen-y-ghent has only me; and the difference in magnitude is about the same between us!

Despite the Yorkshire habit of "cutting things down to size" I insist on calling it a mountain and not a hill. Pen-y-ghent looks like a mountain because it rises, like a crouching lion — almost a natural sphinx — from a relatively level piece of fell. It is noble and dignified but eminently approachable. There are many routes to the top and, in fact, the Pennine Way goes up one side, across the summit and down the other.

We climbed it often and in all weathers. Two occasions separated by something like forty years stand out. The first was about 1958 or '59. My wife and I were both young and fit and we had two daughters under three. During a hot dry spell of weather we set off from home pushing a high coach-built pram. The younger girl lay in the pram; the older sat on a makeshift seat across it. Tucked into the bottom boards was a kettle, kindling and the wherewithal to make tea. We also had sandwiches and cake. We set off. At first the route was easy, then we got onto a greenway (an old drovers' road) and the track was rough. Luckily a prolonged dry spell had hardened the way and we didn't get bogged down. We manhandled that pram over stiles, across drystone walls and soon began to climb at an angle which made it safer for one child to walk and the other to be carried turn and turn about. Eventually the pram would go no higher. We stopped, rummaged in the bottom for fuel and water (sealed into a camping kettle with a screw spout) and brewed-up. That was possibly the best flavoured cup of tea I have ever tasted. The sandwiches, too, were superb even if they were mundane beef paste or cheese.

We poured the rest of the water onto the fire to make certain it was out. We had a reserve bottle for later and repacked the pram tidily. From there it was onwards and upwards, struggling in places, scrambling in others; we shared the children between us and we made it to the top. The view was magnificent, cloudless and free from the heat haze that so often spoils visibility from "up there". Three of us shared a bar of chocolate and the youngest member of the party had her own refreshment from a bottle.

Back at the pram we drank our water and had a last upward look at where we had been. Then we set off home. And believe me, getting a high coach-built pram DOWN a rugged track is a whole lot harder than getting the same vehicle up.

Only a couple of years ago those same daughters along with their younger brother joined together to give us a special wedding anniversary present: a week in a holiday cottage in the same village and a hamper of the most extravagant food and drink anyone could imagine.

We had a truly wonderful time and completely indulged ourselves. We spent most evenings and much of every day in re-living those glorious years when we called the area home.

We had, of course, to climb Pen-y-ghent, even though arthritis and other conditions that hamper movement in old age, made it a long, slow process. We took out time and rested whenever we wanted to. We had nothing to prove and cheerfully returned the greetings and good wishes of other climbers. Half way up we stopped for lunch. No fires this time. We drank from flasks and enjoyed our sandwiches, thinking about the last time we had done this all those years before. My wife took another sandwich and suddenly giggled. "I wonder how many people before us have sat here eating smoked salmon sandwiches made with home-made brown bread". The improbability of the situation and the incongruousness of such an archetypal "county" sandwich on a rugged Pennine mountainside, reduced me to giggles also. No-one else would have thought the situation funny and it is impossible to explain it. It is the kind of silly humour that only really works between people who have been married nearly fifty years.

We got back to the car after an excursion of a little over 3 hours: which is not far off the time it took the champion fell-runner to do all Three Peaks in the annual race.

Ah well!

Progress?

It stands proud and tall. It towers over the surrounding property like some giant Freudian symbol. It is Lister's Mill chimney in Manningham, Bradford. Lister's Mill, or Manningham Mills to give its correct title, is something of an icon in the textile world. The chimney, for example, is reputed to be wide enough round the top for a coach and four horses to be driven round.

Its fame was entirely due to its output of knitting yarn of every possible kind. And whether they knew it or not, all of the thousands of knitters in all parts of the United Kingdom, were responsible for its on-going success. However, people hardly ever knit any more. Knitting wool is passé and the fame of Lister's Mill is history already. Anachronistic it may be, useless in a modern context but nevertheless a tribute to, indeed a symbol of, the Industrial Revolution at its most splendid.

Lister's Mill chimney synthesises all the elements that turned rural Britain into urban slum and transcends them all. It is visible from the surrounding moors; a giant amongst lesser columns which together, provide the Industrial Revolution's response to religion and the churches that represent it.

This is visible history. We look at the past and are repelled by it, or admire it according to our point of view. But history is not simply what we read about, or see around us. It engages the other senses too.

My wife, when young, would often visit the mill of which her father was manager and help him to oversee — and often to strip down and clean — the huge flat bedded steam engines that operated the looms. For her the Industrial Revolution becomes the sound of clattering moving parts and the smell of engine oil. Only once did I ever see her display this engineering expertise. It was some forty years later. We were on holiday in Ulverston and visited a bobbin mill. Indeed it was one of the last bobbin mills ever to produce those finely twisted wooden cylinders upon which spun yard is wound.

The mill was really a working museum and the day we visited, it was virtually deserted. One solitary employee remained. He showed us round with not much enthusiasm until we reached the engine room. There, in the process of being cleaned was a small, gleaming flatbed steam engine. All polished brass and glistening oil. My wife exclaimed and recognised the make and provenance of the machine. The effect on our guide was astounding. All his rather desultory guide-speak disappeared in an instant. He and my wife entered into a highly technical conversation which clearly delighted them both.

I was ignored and spent my time exploring the workrooms examining bobbins in all stages of manufacture. I enjoyed the smell of the wood, the texture of its surface and the associations it had of plantations of growing trees. This was my world. I was happy to be in it. And the glow of satisfaction in my wife's face as we drove away said it all.

To quote T. S. Eliot, "All this was a long time ago / I remember . . ."

Since we last visited the bobbin mill it may well have closed down. Nowadays synthetic fibres have entirely transformed the textile industry. A chain has been snapped and link by link the livelihood of many generations has ceased to be, except in museums and craft centres. Soon, museums too will lack viability. They will close. And, at considerably less cost, it will all be available as virtual reality on computer. But I wonder how long it will take virtual reality to catch up with Huxley's *Brave New World*?

We already have visual, auditory and tactile interaction. How long before we can also experience synthetic smell and taste?

We started with a symbol of 19th century might and grandeur, we moved on to more recent things and ended with virtual reality. Even now — and it was rumoured several years ago — Lister's Mill chimney may be felled like a forest tree and exist no more except in memory.

One thing this changing world of ours has taught me as I reminisce about places I have lived in and loved.

It is always a mistake to go back.

Ribblehead

Coming from Hawes you see it straddling the road just beyond the left turn to Selside, Horton and, eventually Settle.

Although it is neither rose-red nor half as old as time, Ribblehead Viaduct stands, imperiously, like some great gateway into a fortress. The entire structure is an enigma. In the broad light of a summer's day it has solidity; it is a monument to man's indomitable power in taking tons of dull grey stone and converting it into something, if not beautiful, of grandeur and utility.

All this was done at a cost: the cost of dozens of lives. The evidence for this lies in the churchyard of Chapel-Le-Dale some three miles down the road to Ingleton.

But none of this troubles the children who play on the edge of the moorland. Protected by cars and comforted by the presence of an ice-cream van, young and old alike can relax and engage in simple games in and out of the beck. Or they can simply look out towards the comforting presence of Pen-y-ghent and promise themselves, and even perhaps their children, that one day they would set off from Horton, climb to the top and then go home and say that they've done part of the Pennine Way. And who could blame them?

These are the visitors, the tourists who have a genuine love of wild country: but on their own terms. What about the residents? Those of us who live and work all year round in that exalted region. I mean the farmers, the stockmen and shepherds. By contrast the quarrymen and their families. Yes; and those, too, who serve their needs. I mean the publicans, the schoolteachers, the district nurses and the blacksmiths. All of them dedicated to staying alive and handing on their property and services when the time comes for them to join that band of navvies who gave their all without thought of perpetuity.

Such thoughts occur whenever I drive up the road from Ingleton to Ribblehead. Past White Scar Caves on the right and Chapel-Le-Dale churchyard on the left. It is a switchback of a road, rising and falling in a sequence of crests and troughs always rising upwards.

Our children, when young, used to love that road and, for their delight we would often go that way home even if it was a roundabout way.

As one would expect, with such a history the area is supposed to be haunted. I am totally agnostic as far as ghosts are concerned but one night I was almost persuaded.

It was late Autumn and late at night. We were going home from a day out at Kendal and we took "the back way". As so often happens in Autumn, especially in areas where the rock types are contrasted — limestone and millstone grit for example — curious air currents create localised patches of fog.

I knew this, of course, intellectually. But it did nothing for my blood pressure as we passed Chapel-Le-Dale and on up to Ribblehead, to be accompanied by wraiths of mist that, increasingly, as we travelled, looked like shrouds.

You Heard it Here First

What would you do if you were accosted one morning with the shouted comment: "A mister, yan o't'gimmers is rig-welted"?

A fellowship of the Institute of Linguists might not help. Membership of the Yorkshire Dialect Society could well provide a clue. But if you were a hill shepherd you would not even think academically. You would pull on your wellies, get your warmest clothing on and dash out.

A gimmer is a female sheep between 1 and 2 years old. Being rig-welted means lying on your back unable to get up. If a sheep falls into a ditch and rolls onto its back it is literally unable to do anything about it. If left it will die of starvation and exposure.

I love all accents and dialects and the language of the fell farmers, imbued as it is with Old Norse, makes it a joy to listen to. in fact, it is rumoured that during the early years of the war, when there was something of a news blackout from Westminster, Dales farmers of an older generation would listen in to their antiquated radios. By tuning to the Norwegian news stations they often gained at least a day or two on the rest of the population as far as war intelligence was concerned.

163

It must be obvious that language, especially etymology, is my life's study. I particularly enjoy teasing out the many stranded meanings and derivations that exist in place-names and the specific, often regional, names that are given to farming tools and livestock.

I mentioned gimmer above. This is a very specific title in the shepherd's vocabulary. In the naming of sheep I am reminded that in the Inuit language there are very many words for snow. It's the same with shepherding. If you wish to be persona grata around the auction rings and salegrounds of the North you have to know your gimmer hogg from your wether hogg and, especially if you want to go into the sheep breeding business, you have to be able to distinguish both from a tup hogg.

It's simple really once you have grasped the fact that hogg with two g's is a sheep: with only one it is a pig. The life history of sheep is as follows. It starts off as a lamb until it is weaned (or spained in the case of sheep). Once separated from its mother it becomes a hogg. It is a gimmer hogg (female), a wether hogg (castrated male) or a tup hogg (an entire male kept for breeding).

The rest of the life cycle refers to the annual clippings. The first clipping is a shearling. Subsequently with each year the name depends upon the fact that two teeth are grown annually until at four shears the animal is fully adult or "full mouth".

And if you think that is bizarre you ought to look into the traditional methods of counting as they were once applied. It is impossible here to do justice to this linguistic phenomenon because each separate dale has its own vocabulary, and the Lake District another.

It may have emerged from this that I am passionate about sheep as well as language. It may therefore be appropriate, in view of my already declared interest in horse racing, to give the shortened etymology of the town of Wetherby. You may well have worked it out already.

WETHERBY . . . Wether (a castrated male of the first year) + by (Old Norse for farm). Curiously enough, the name in its present form did not appear until 1238. The Domesday Book has it recorded as Wedrebi.

Those Ruddy Ducks

I do not usually take up arms against people whose opinions differ from my own. If a person has moral or ethical objections to fox hunting for example I would not wish to restrain them or challenge their right to speak. Even if I had the previous night sustained the total loss of a — free range — flock of chickens owing to vulpine vandalism: I would still let them have their say.

That being so, I do feel that objections should be based upon informed criticism and not emotional gut-feeling (or maybe sheer mischief-making as I suppose some of the protests to be).

To be topical, why are the members of the organisation Animal Aid alarmed at the R.S.P.B. supporting a controlled cull of the Ruddy Ducks? This, on general admission, is an unwanted input from America which is disturbing the European ecology by occupying niches previously held by native species. This is another example of a circumstance when interference by man, for some reason of his own, profoundly disturbs the natural order of things.

This situation arose when the grey squirrel took over and virtually banished our native red (in much the same way as waves of Roman and Saxon invaders banished the Celtic Britons). It happened again when

166

the coypu — bred for its fur, called nutria — was allowed to escape into the waterways of East Anglia and totally devastated vegetation, both natural and garden, in addition to destroying the river banks by burrowing holes. More recently the mink is upsetting the riverways and even displacing the otter in some areas. And we all love the otter, don't we?

In the end it all comes back to what is described in simple terms as the "balance of nature".

Every habitat is a fine balance — a natural balance — between member species. It is an over simplification to talk about food chains as if there is only one line of development. The expression food web is much more suitable.

The main problem for the complainants is their inability to see the situation as a whole, coupled with a tendency to anthropomorphism. Let us try to humanise the situation by using a parable in human terms.

There was once a village in East Yorkshire. It had all the attributes for which the English village is renowned: quaint cottages, stone built and slated; a village green with a pond and a village pump. Most of the villagers either worked on farms or had some connection with the land. The others ran the shop & Post Office, the bakery, the smithy and the saddler who also made and repaired boots and shoes. There was a school, a church and a lock-up surgery which a doctor from the local town visited once a week. The town was something like ten miles away. Half of the land belonged to the estate of the Lord of the Manor; the remainder belonged to tenant farmers or owner occupiers.

For hundreds of years the village thrived through good times and bad. People helped each other.

Wars came and went: fortunes and property changed hands; most of all technology enhanced production at the expense of manpower. Young people — out of work young people — drifted away to the towns in search of work. The cottages they might have lived in were sold off to town dwellers who either commuted from them or used them simply as weekend retreats. The incomers brought with them goods from the supermarkets: the village shop could not compete. The smithy — once it had satisfied the demand for wrought iron gates — became a filling station and garage. Only the estate land held out against the foreign invasion until the old squire died.

His only son was a chartered accountant in the city, many miles away. He sold out the estate land to a property developer who contracted to build an estate of houses and hostels to expand the accommodation for staff and students at the nearby university.

One thing remained of the old village: the Drovers Rest. It was a pub that had served countless generations of locals and itinerate cattlemen. It was long and low and had a yard for horses and a pound for beasts going to market.

That, too, succumbed to the developers. A nationwide brewery chain bought it, gutted it and transformed it by every "Ye Olde" means in the book.

And to show their country connections they renamed it The Ruddy Duck.

The Champion

As a young teacher (and later a college lecturer) I took advantage of the long holidays to do a range of holiday jobs. This was partly for the extra cash but mainly for the wider experience I could get by doing manual rather than intellectual things. In this way I was, by turns, a bencher-up on a building site, a conductor on the local buses and a kennel worker at a quarantine kennels. Most memorably I became a minder at a bull-farm — or artificial insemination centre. For this I worked, not only for the long vacation, but some weekends for much of the rest of the year as a casual stand-in. Because of this I was involved in what follows and not simply a second-hand reporter.

Under the general management of a Regional Veterinary Officer an A.I. centre employs a wide range of staff. The actual inseminators who go out to farmers and inseminate cows either with semen from a nominated bull, or more cheaply, with the services of the "bull of the day". Also the scientific staff there are the laboratory workers who perform viability tests and also maintain the strictest of controls over the storage of the semen in tubes plunged into liquid nitrogen.

There are also assistant or trainee field members and a host of maintenance staff who maintain the centre's efficiency and see to the welfare of the bovine inmates. I was in this — the lowest rung on the ladder, although I was given opportunities to learn beyond my station, because of a mistaken belief that I was a student veterinary doing course work in the field.

This is hardly the place for me to expound the technicalities or the mechanics of insemination. It is enough to say that what seems bizarre at the beginning rapidly became commonplace, and within a week both the techniques and the vocabulary that describes them were taken for granted.

No, what impressed me were characters of the bulls on the one hand and the temperaments and personalities of those "minders" on the other.

Bulls are incalculable creatures. Appearances are deceptive. The largest, most cumbersome and fearsome looking are usually placid and even affectionate. Indeed, one lordly specimen — a Friesian from the renowned Terling line — was reputed to be so biddable that the R.V.O's children could take rides on his back.

By contrast the most aggressive, vicious and totally untamed are usually the Channel Island breeds. Who could imagine it when looking at a herd of Jersey cows, that they (placid and wonderfully friendly to all) could have been sired by an animal that would try every dodge to get the better of his keepers and always be ready to thrust his lethal horns at the most vulnerable parts of the human anatomy.

Such a beast is the hero of this tale: an example of the sentimental epithet "Love conquers all". He was a member of the illustrious Groombridge line with an auspicious pedigree that recorded several generations of true breeding and continuing excellence. His prowess as a progenitor — a stud bull which consistently sired heifers of the highest quality — was formidable and he was much in demand. The only problem was that he was sullen, fierce and, when the black mood took him, totally unusable. His pet name was Satan.

If Satan is the hero of this tale, the heroine was slim, blonde and deceptively demure. She was called Emma and, at the time, just 18.

Emma joined the staff much as I had done, for the experience. There the resemblance ended. Since leaving school at 16, Emma had already had two jobs. Her first had been as a kennel maid; her second as a stable girl at a nearby equestrian centre. Each had lasted just a year and from both she had emerged with praise for her skill and dedication. It was not fickleness or a restless nature that saw Emma in her third job in three years. It was her own, personal, way of getting experience or field work to back up her burning ambition to be a veterinary nurse: a farm veterinary nurse she would always add, not a practice that specialised in dogs, cats and budgies.

To say that, almost instantly, Emma fell in love with Satan would be absurd. She was fascinated by him. She listened to all the lurid tales (and everyone who had anything to do with the old devil had at least one such) and made up her mind that she would befriend him.

Satan got his exercise by being attached to a heavy duty roundabout, similar to the clothes drying frames to be found in gardens. To get him from his stall to the roundabout was usually a two-man job: a very sensitive two man job. Once attached to the roundabout he was relatively safe because, unlike stallions, bulls cannot kick backwards.

Emma stopped coming to the staff room at lunch break. Nobody thought much of this since lunch breaks were staggered and extended over about two and a half hours. Emma had decided to take her sandwiches down to the exercise frame and "talk" to Satan during her break. We left her to it.

Because Emma and I were temporary staff we each had a bi-monthly commitment to get out to farms with an inseminator. For some reason which escapes me I needed to swap my visit and went down to the exercise area to ask her. As I arrived I heard voices.

"Come on, you silly old fool. Stand still! I can't reach that high; not without getting on a box or — There now! just look what you've done. All over my jeans."

I emerged to see a flustered Emma, empty bucket in hand with water swirling around her. She had been grooming Satan.

After that I often went down to the exercise area when Emma was there. I took my own sandwiches. I did not go to chat with Emma but simply to watch her in action. She was a marvel. She had Satan literally eating out of her hand.

This liaison inevitably came to the notice of the Regional Veterinary Officer. The R.V.O was the official administrator and the centre was run on impeccable lines, thanks to his secretary who had a flair for details to soothe the bureaucratic breast. The old man was thus left free to do what he did best: attend to the welfare of the animals.

Emma had always been a favourite of his — perhaps a substitute for the daughter he had never had. The Old Man's family were three boys all rough, tough rugger playing characters, copies of himself.

How she did it none of us ever knew, but Emma, all through an early autumn to late winter had persevered and Satan was, not a reformed character, but biddable and workable so long as Emma was there at his head. And then she dropped her bombshell. The Old Man was not a democratic individual by any means but he called an ad hoc staff meeting and announced that Emma had asked him point blank if she might enter Satan for the Great Yorkshire Show. What did we think? Emma and I being temporary staff had no say in the matter. We supervised the yard whilst the staff deliberated.

"He's got to do it you know!" Emma spoke with unaccustomed passion.

"Be honest, Em," I tried not to sound patronising, "the Old Man has got the responsibility for the Centre — the entire service — riding on his shoulders."

"Oh, I know, but it's the chance of a lifetime, it is." Emma's Irish origins became more obvious the more impassioned she became. "Are you with me, or against me?" she demanded.

173

"No-one's against you Em. It's just that some old hands think it a —"

"A crackpot idea? Maybe it is; but he'll win if he gets there."

"Maybe . . . but how can you be so sure?"

"Because I've read the breed requirements 'til I say them in my sleep. I've measured him and matched him up and he fits, I'm telling you. Satan's perfect — I'm telling you!"

Whilst this conversation was going on the rest of the staff deliberated. The voting was tight and the R.V.O got the casting vote.

He voted for Em. She had his blessing to set up the scheme and to prepare Satan for his star part. All this so long as the efficiency of the Centre was in no way diminished.

The number of man hours (perhaps I should say "Em hours") expended in getting the great brute into show condition would have clocked up the biggest overtime bill in the entire country. But for Em giving Satan what is nowadays called a makeover was a labour of love. She even polished his horns and his hooves.

The night before the show opened Satan's transporter and his entourage of Emma and two of the toughest minders left the Centre for Harrogate. So far, so good.

From first light on the morning of what is known as "judgement day" the livestock area of the showground was a never-ending clamour and clatter of activity. Satan stood like a monarch surveying the scene. He was strangely subdued — not tense with anxiety and emotion as we all were who were there to support Emma's enterprise — as if he were entirely switched off.

Throughout all the frenzy of preparation Emma appeared cool and confident; totally at ease. At last the various classes were lined up: breed by breed. There was not a very large entry in the Channel Islands (Jersey) category. Already the Channel Island breeds had become something of a novelty. Gold topped milk with its 6+% butterfat was beginning to be frowned upon by the food faddists.

Satan surveyed his fellow bulls with bovine disdain. He observed the various classes of females (heifers, cows in milk, cows with calf at foot etc) with little or no concern. Perhaps, because of his sheltered upbringing he had no idea what they were. Some may even have been his own progeny.

The parade began, and the line up, and the judging. Satan was on his best behaviour. He was much better mannered even than some of the others. Several of the bulls were accompanied by more than one stockman. How many of them carried — as we did — a gun and tranquillizer darts I cannot say.

Whoever said that fairy tales do not come true, had obviously not met (or even heard of) Emma and Satan; the double act supreme. He took best of breed. We all breathed a sigh of sheer relief and felt suddenly exhausted. Then he was hastily returned to his transporter and taken home — but not before he was suitably photographed and the cup was in the hands of a grateful but still slightly shocked R.V.O.

And Emma — the ice cool tamer of the old monster — how did she feel. She smiled and then her hands twitched and she literally passed out and was restored only to say to everyone "He did it . . . he did it . . . I always knew he would." Over and over again.

Emma had hardly slept for 24 hours and had probably not eaten a serious meal for much longer. She must have been ravenously hungry to have sustained herself on a diet of fingernails for so long.

Shortly after this, our yearly contracts being up, Emma and I left the Centre. I had enjoyed my time there a great deal. Emma achieved much more, as her memories and a folder of cuttings from the *Yorkshire Post*, the *Evening News* and the *Telegraph* and *Argus* would always confirm.

But — and there is always a but even in the most glorious of happenings — the old hero himself, Satan although a reformed character, did not go on to further glories.

The A.I. service had an exchange system whereby bulls are moved about the country from centre to centre. Because of the decline of Jersey herds in Yorkshire it was decided to transfer Satan to another centre in the south, where the demand for his services would be greater.

Travelling on the same transporter as he used on his triumphant journey to Harrogate and back, Satan was sent off down the M1. Somewhere along the stretch between Milton Keynes and Luton there was a collision between a huge tanker and Satan's transporter. The driver of the Land Rover and his companion escaped serious injury. Satan was not so lucky. He had to be put down by the road side: suitably screened against the prying eyes of the passers by. I was upset when I heard about it but I cannot say how Emma reacted. We promised to stay in touch but you know how it is.

The Old Man of the Mountains

There was something enigmatic about him right from the start. I saw him walking up the footpath off Marsett Lane towards the head of the lake. he was dressed casually: good quality Norfolk jacket and breeches in matching tweed. His boots were old fashioned, made for walking and not rock-climbing. In keeping with the rest of his outfit his rucksack was old fashioned; heavy canvas with several side pockets. He walked with a slow, purposeful and persistent stride that would keep him going all day.

I had just completed a circuit of Semerwater. I was sitting by a wall, sheltered from the wind, eating my sandwiches and drinking coffee from a flask. My wife, who normally walks with me, had had to go into Hawes for the day and she was due to pick me up in about half an hour. I watched the man until he was almost level but he gave little indication that he was aware of my scrutiny.

I raised my Thermos and said: "Want some?"

He stopped. "Thank you; that's most kind." The voice was educated but rather stilted — as if he wasn't

178

used to being accosted by total strangers. He accepted the coffee from the inner thermos top.

We sat together, side by side, looking out over Semerwater. The sky was a milky blue, the sun was slanting across our angle of view and the water looked slightly rippled with just a hint here and there of miniature white horses.

There was no need for conversation and the silence was companionable. Then: "I suppose you know the legend?" I nodded.

The old story tells of a prosperous settlement unknowable years ago which denied hospitality to a vagrant. Nobody would offer him either food or drink and shelter was denied him in all but a remote tenant's cottage. That night the old man stood at the cottage door and called down a curse upon the place:

"Semerwater rise, Semerwater sink,
And swallow all the town save this little house,
Where they gave me food and drink."

That night a deluge drowned the prosperous place for ever.

"Are you a superstitious man?" My companion's voice broke in upon my thoughts.

"Not particularly. Why?" He had clearly been reading my thoughts. I dispensed the last of the coffee and he took out a pipe and pouch. When the tobacco was burning to his satisfaction, he answered.

"There are a lot of wild tales. It is possible, just possible, that there was a prehistoric lake dwelling on piles. Got destroyed." As he became engrossed in his tale, his speech became elliptical: almost as if he was talking to himself. He smiled in silence for a while and then said: "Have you ever heard of Talkin Tarn?"

"No", I replied.

"About 7 miles from Carlisle." He thought for a moment. "Same story; inhospitable residents, old man turned away. Now comes the variation. The vagrant fell down on his knees at the centre of the village and prayed for retribution. That night there was torrential rain, earthquake and the total loss of the village."

Something stirred in my memory. I was told a similar tale when I was staying at Cartmel some years earlier. "Urswick Lake". The laconic style of conversation was infectious.

"Exactly. There really were earthquakes in that area centuries ago." He re-lit his pipe.

I could not resist saying that there was no earthquake in the Semerwater story.

"True", a further pause. He looked out over the surface of the water and said, "Semerwater. That's a triple tautology." The change of subject jarred my mind for a moment until the puzzle became clear: in Old English sae = lake; mere = pool; and water, gives us water, water, water.

"Like Pendle Hill," I replied, trying to be equally enigmatic.

"Almost. But Pen is Celtic; Hyll is Old English. It's a cross fertilization."

I watched my wife drive into the car park and stood up. "Can we drop you anywhere?"

He shook his head. "Thank you, but no. I'm walking across to Burtersett. Bed and breakfast." He wriggled into his rucksack and shrugged it into a comfortable position. Then he was off: same pace, same stride. It was as if he'd never stopped in the first place.

"Who on earth was that?" My wife had walked across to where I stood watching my erstwhile companion.

"Oh, just someone who stopped by. Scholarly sort of chap." We drove off, and that was that. Until Friday. On the page where the local correspondents have their columns there was a photograph. Same chap. Underneath the photograph was written: Professor Lewis Graves, renowned authority on Anglo-Saxon settlements and languages, addressed the English Place-names Society at their conference at Malham Tarn Field Study Centre. The report went into details and included the information that Professor Graves was doing field work in the area whilst researching a forthcoming book.

That chance meeting set me thinking about legends in general and these ones in particular. Just as an unsolved crossword clue will send the mind to and fro in search of a solution, this problem triggered an urge in me to unravel not just why those legends exist but how (or who) started them in the first place?

All in a Day's Work

Hugh Metcalfe was a third generation Dales farmer. I knew him first through his son Arthur, whom I taught for a couple of years. Arthur's sole ambition was to leave school as soon as possible and establish himself as a dry stone waller. He was bright, lively but entirely "non-academic". It was my job to "put some learnin' into him".

Once a week, therefore, I walked up the unmade farm track — that had once been a drovers' road — and sat down in the "front room" with a pile of books and a reluctant Arthur.

Almost in spite of himself Arthur began to learn. So much so, in fact, that he began to tell me at school things he had read in the *Farmer & Stockbreeder*. One day he came to me and said that his Dad would like a word when it was "handy like". Then the truth came out: Hugh Metcalfe couldn't read — at least not very well. And would I mind . . . ?"

This began a curious relationship. Once a week I'd go up to the farm and teach Hugh. He was so determined that he made astounding progress. In addition to the lessons we shared, I shared something of his life and aspirations too.

182

Hugh's grandfather had been a traditional Dales farmer of the kind James Herriot wrote about: taciturn, shrewd and single-minded. He used his open fell to rear sheep — Dalesbred to be precise — in their hundreds. He also had a small amount of meadow land in the Dale bottom and he cropped it for hay. In a small pasture near the farm he kept a house-cow.

Hugh's father was a slightly more sophisticated version of grandfather. He ran fewer sheep, took in and improved more pasture and meadow and had a tidy beef herd which almost ran itself.

Hugh himself, as a lad, took the beef unit off his father's hands, introduced more dairy beasts and soon became the first farmer in the dale to use the Milk Marketing Board's Artificial Insemination Service. His venture flourished but his education was sorely neglected. In those days, farm children, were allowed certain weeks off school; for lambing, harvesting, and hay time. Hugh and his Dad took full advantage of this; and then some more.

When it was his turn to farm in his own right, Hugh made dramatic changes. He rented out all of his fell to sheep men and specialised in a high class Friesian dairy herd of his own, with bought-in Dale bottom pasture.

We became very close. After I had done as much for him as I could in teaching him to read, I continued to visit the farm and helped out with the milking.

With his new-found literacy skills, Hugh read farming books, journals and newspapers. He visited shows and exhibitions and became the very first farmer in the entire Dale to install a turntable milking parlour.

183

The cows arrived from the holding yard, took up their places with placid expectation until the unit was full. Their tag numbers were entered and by some mysterious computerised technique, the correct amount of highly concentrated food was delivered to their bowls. The milking cups were connected and off they went. The food was eaten, the milk delivered into a static tank and the cows then went out to another yard and the whole process was repeated until the herd had been milked. This happened three times every day.

I was fascinated. I helped out and even did the job on my own when the family went to a show or something. Then came the ultimate in trust.

I had a message from Hugh on Wednesday. If I'd nowt on at weekend would I do him a favour. His wife's brother, who farmed at Oakenclough just south of Lancaster, had invited the family over for the weekend. Would I do the milking and just see things were right. "Just for a couple of nights like." It was then that I discovered Hugh's other passion: snooker. His brother-on-law had been given tickets for the championship at Preston.

I said yes, of course.

I took my duties very seriously and to prevent a journey back and forth three times a day I took up Hugh's offer of a bed so I might be on hand "if owt turned up". This sounded an alarm bell and I said: "I've milked time and again Hugh. What's likely to turn up?"

"Well," he looked slightly shamefaced. "There's that heifer's due to calve. It's her first, like, and she ought to be kept an eye on."

I helped with Friday's milking, Hugh and family set off and my wife and I were left in charge. Other people's houses, especially those about 250 years old, bring out all the superstitious feelings that lie only just below the surface. We sat and read and played cribbage. Eventually I said that I'd go and look at the heifer and just check round before we turned in. The heifer seemed in good condition and not in any imminent danger of calving.

Saturday came in, bright and cheerful. The morning milking went off without a hitch, but the heifer looked to be somewhat stressed. I rang the vet.

He came and performed a fairly difficult delivery. I helped as well as I could; which is another way of saying I pulled when I was told to pull and relaxed when I was told to relax. I don't know how the heifer felt, but I was exhausted. Her problem was the size of the calf's head and other complications which I am not competent to deal with. I thanked the vet and rang Hugh's brother-in-law's farm. I told Hugh the outcome. I tried to sound nonchalant but something in my voice gave away that underneath I was slightly anxious.

"Is owt wrong?"

I didn't even hesitate. "No, I'm O.K. It's just, well, someone else's heifer and someone else's farm." There was silence for a moment. Then: "I'll tell thee what. I'd never have trusted you without thinking you'd 'andle t'job." I was much relieved and rang off.

Later that evening the heifer seemed suddenly to wilt, to buckle at the knees. I rang the vet again. I told him the symptoms and he seemed to arrive almost as soon as I'd put the phone down. One injection of calcium later and the heifer was contentedly suckling her calf.

"Milk fever", said the vet. "Quite common in heifers especially when she's had a bit of a struggle." He went on to explain that it was a serious lack of calcium. "In the old days, it wasn't so easy. We had to use a bicycle pump to blow up the udder". He got up to go. "I shouldn't bother Hugh 'til he gets back. She'll be O.K., just keep an eye on her."

I was late to bed and dreamed fitfully of calcium and bicycle pumps and calves that were inflated: floating around the calving stall like great grotesque balloons.

The phone rang. It was just after midnight. Hugh; a jubilant and exultant Hugh.

"Ah thought tha'd like to know. Terry Griffiths has just got a 147".

What could I say?

Snow

During the six months or so that we had lived in the fellside cottage, the late night walk had become a ritual. It exercised the dog. It enabled me to check up on the hen house and the goose pen. It also gave me the chance to look about me; across the dale to the other fellside; up and down the narrow road, to the village one way, and towards the main road the other. And most of all to confirm how grateful I was to live in such a glorious place.

My last act before going to bed was to riddle out the Aga and re-charge it with a layer of coalite and then top it up with logs.

On the night I have in mind there was something different about the place. It was composed of stillness and silence. It was also freezing sharp. There was anticipation, like waiting for the first strike of midnight on New Year's Eve. To add to the unusualness, the Aga — normally a biddable creature — proved stubborn, went out and then refused to draw because of an almost total lack of movement in the air.

I emptied the Aga and started again. This time, with persuasion, it began to draw. I loaded it in the usual way and damped it right down. As I took out the ashes

I noticed that the stillness had gone. There was a sharpish breeze and as I refilled the log basket from the shed I was aware of a drift of snow flakes like a cloud of gnats between myself and the light from the kitchen door.

I woke to a world transformed. During the night my "sharpish breeze" had become a steady blow and there were drifts across the lane up to the tops of the walls. The sky was still overcast and snow fell, but there was a colour change in the sky, from the deep indigo to a sickly orangy-yellow. The sun was doing its best.

There was a sudden break. Miraculously the clouds burned away and the entire landscape shimmered with diamond brightness and shades of blue. I'd read about this effect but had never seen it with such clarity and vividness.

For all its beauty it nevertheless meant work: hard physical work. I cleared a path to the shed and carried on around the house from the kitchen to the gate. By this time the farmer from further down the lane had fired up his ancient Fordson Major and attached it to the cumbersome snow plough that stood upright against the barn for the rest of the year. The lane was quickly cleared. Unfortunately, the bow wave of snow splayed out and covered the path that I had dug earlier. However, the exercise did me good and the setter didn't mind a bit. After romping like a puppy in the deepest drifts, biting the snow and tossing it about, he paused only long enough to bite the icicles from his leg feathers before rejoining the fray.

Later I joined the Fordson Major (snowplough in front and trailer behind) and all of us, farmer, self and two dogs set off down the road and across to the opposite side of the fell. From the barn we loaded hay bales and took them up the fellside for the out-wintering stirks. We broke the ice in the water troughs. We went even higher to see to the sheep.

We worked all day and all day it froze: by nightfall the once pristine snowscape was rutted and pitted as every farmer in the dale had done what we had been doing whilst the light held.

That night the frost went on but no more snow. We watched the news and, as always, were amazed by the chaos that a fairly modest fall of snow could cause to the roads and pavements of our major cities. They had no more snow than us, probably less. But they floundered: we coped.

Later we went outside and looked across the dale to where we had worked all day. Under a clear sky and a three-quarter moon the snow glistened. It was as if it gave out its own icy luminosity. One by one we noted the pin-prick windows of the scattered farmsteads across the fells. They were all accounted for and no "black hole" suggested damaged power lines. We were all safe.

Being tired but not sleepy I left replenishing the Aga until the latest possible hour and then sat enjoying the warmth and thinking about all the books where a snow storm provides the pivotal point in the plot. I singled out the "Snow" chapter of Arthur Ransome's *Winter Holiday*; I dipped into the "Snow" section of the *Magic*

Mountain by Thomas Mann — a monumental book from every point of view. I began to re-read *The Dead* by James Joyce and once again became hooked and read on to the final poignant paragraph. But most of all I read again some of the snow scenes from *Diary of a Country Parson* by James Woodforde.

As I drifted into sleep I pondered the contrast between literary snow and the real thing. I was faintly aware that the wind had risen once again.

Fresh falls that night and the night after freshened up the landscape but did little to disrupt the day to day comings and goings. Cows were milked and the heavy stainless steel churns (or kits) were put out for collection. Stock were fed and water troughs replenished. Wild birds welcomed the grain and bread crumbs and we daily totted up the spoors of animals that came and went by night. We also saw the crimson stains on the snow where foxes and stoats had got the better of rabbits and smaller rodents, made less cautious by the hardness of the weather.

The dale took on a self-sufficiency and we "saw it out" with a minimum of fuss from the outside world. By almost telepathic means we helped each other out. The highlight of the siege was the second midnight when young Mrs Moorby up at Grange Farm went into labour — her first. It was naturally a private, almost domestic, event but everyone in the dale knew by morning — especially after the postman had done his round.

It all ended, as suddenly as it began, after five days. But the ending was remarkable for a phenomenon that I had read about but never before experienced.

Most days, towards late afternoon, there had been a slight thaw followed, after sunset, by further frost. This crisped up the snow's surface to a perilous slipperiness. This time it was different: thaw, freeze and then the sky clouded over in a manner that suggested more snow. But no! The great thaw had begun. However, before the snow became porous, before the bite of the frost finally left, a curious circumstance occurred. It was like the Whispering Gallery at St Paul's Cathedral.

Voices, normally pitched voices, could be heard across the dale from side to side. Personal conversations were transmitted by a combination of cloud cover, frozen snow and the atmospheric density. It seemed as if conversations were "bounced off" the clouds, reflected back from the still icy snow and thus bounced across the best part of a mile.

Just think: if Mrs Moorby had hung on for a couple of days longer, the postman would have been pre-empted.

A Sting in the Tale

When faced with any unpleasant decision, be it Northern Ireland or the state of the economy, someone in the public eye is bound to trot out "we must simply grasp the nettle." The meaning is obvious: to take on an unpleasant task or confront a seemingly insoluble problem. It is part of every politician's verbal armoury like "at the end of the day" or "in the long term".

Of course, the common nettle is not called stinging nettle for nothing. Anyone who has grown up a country child will remember the pain and anguish of running incautiously after a ball into a patch of hedgerow vegetation, or along the headland of a grazing field. The speedy application of a dock leaf well lubricated with saliva was the only chance of relief — and even that may have been psychological rather than practical treatment.

Why then should "grasping the nettle" be an efficacious way of solving life's real problems? Some will tell you that grasping a nettle firmly rather than brushing lightly against it, fails to release the dreaded formic acid. I've never been brave enough to put this to the test. I prefer to accept what has always been an old (a very old) family belief: that a person could be cured of a fever by pulling up nettles with bare hands.

In the North of England at least, the nettle needs no rehabilitation. It has never been out of favour. In the North, nettle beer, nettle tea, young nettles eaten in salads or cooked as an alternative to spinach are all commonplace. The plant is rich in minerals and certain vitamins. It has also been cultivated as a crop to supply cholorophyll to the pharmaceutical chemist. All good practical uses for a much vilified wild plant.

Like most wild plants of great antiquity, folklore has invested the stinging nettle with many and various qualities. The seeds are allegedly an aphrodisiac; the stem fibres were once used, like flax, to be twisted into thread and woven into cloth. The ancient Greeks, ever aware of unusual qualities, were said to use nettles to cure snake bites and scorpion stings — by a kind of sympathetic magic one must suppose. But why was the nettle ever used as an antidote for hemlock poisoning and who was ever brave enough, or curious enough, to put it to the test?

By mediaeval times the practical had given way to the fanciful. Anointing the hands with a mixture of house leek juice and nettle venom was supposed to attract fish. How, or why, I cannot say. Again, throwing a bunch of nettles onto the fire in a thunderstorm was thought to deflect lightning. More realistically, bunches of dried nettles hung in kitchen or pantry would deter flies but improbably, bunches near to bee-hives were thought to drive away frogs. But why did anyone ever relate one to the other in these parallels?

193

This is not scepticism but healthy curiosity. I have lived long enough in rural England never to doubt for very long the basic truth that lies behind so many "old wives' tales".

You Can Take It With You

The popular expression "You can't take it with you" is usually used by the cynic in relation to killing oneself with work in order to amass money. There is, however, another way of looking at it.

When we first went to live in the Three Peaks Country we did not have a car. This did not seriously inhibit us. In those days there was a good reliable bus service. It not only served the main roads and towns: the familiar orange and black buses soon became a familiar sight around the villages and minor roads. Indeed, the regular drivers would often go out of their way to pick up elderly or infirm passengers and go to no end of trouble to deliver parcels. In spite of this, they still managed to run to a tight timetable.

Where buses didn't (or couldn't) run we made do with bicycles or on foot.

This rather lengthy introduction is to explain why we did not travel over to Hawes, via Ribblehead, until some time after we had settled down. And it is important to realise this if the full impact of my story is to be appreciated.

* * *

Indulging ourselves in our first car, we were returning home from Hawes one glowing autumn day. On the road between Selside and Horton-in-Ribblesdale, a road which twists and turns, we were suddenly confronted with a peculiarly angled view of Pen-y-ghent. There were the improved pastures, cut into tidy rectangles by dry-stone walls, a farm, its buildings and a cluster of protective trees. And then, in the distance, the great sphinx-like shape of Pen-y-ghent. That instant I had a fit of deja vu. I'd seen it all before, from that very spot with the light coming from just that angle.

Of course I was mistaken. Even as a child I had never been that way before. But I knew it. It was a scene I had looked at before: in a dream perhaps, in another world even?

I am not superstitious. My imagination is not a romantic faculty. I puzzled and then shrugged off the memory on the principle that if I "forgot about it" my unconscious mind would go on working and come up with the answer.

And that is exactly what happened.

I woke suddenly: not in a gentle manner but all of a piece, as a cat or a dog wakes up, fully alert. I knew! It was deja vu of a kind but it was a fully explicable kind.

My Uncle Graham had worked for an auctioneer. As a boy, growing up in Norfolk, I would sometimes go with him, during the school holidays, when he went out valuing property for the saleroom. One visit took us into a village somewhere between Loddon and Beccles. We went to an old rectory, no longer lived in by the clergy, that was being sold up because the elderly widow could no longer live on her own.

It was a sad occasion. The valuation went on and I spent most of my time looking at the books that were piled up high on the floor. A few novels, some classics like Dickens and Walter Scott, but mainly books of science and natural history. The widow saw me looking at these.

"Do you like nature then?" she had the merest trace of a Norfolk accent.

"Yes, I do. I like it a lot."

"Then come you up here with me". Painfully on arthritic legs, she climbed the back stairs. "Go you on ahead right to the top. But don't go in 'til I get there, mind."

I did as I was told and waited impatiently, envious and slightly fearful of what might lay behind that door. Whatever I had imagined I did not expect what I saw.

It was a narrow attic room. At the far end, modelled in cardboard, was the outline of a strangely shaped mountain. In the foreground there were walls, fields and open countryside. A modelled farm house and buildings occupied the left hand corner.

Scattered about the landscape there were sheep and other animals. Two ravens were suspended from the ceiling and a curlew stood imperiously on a wall.

Exactly what my expression was I cannot say. Whether or not I gasped or spoke I do not remember. The old lady relished my reaction and gently, eyes

197

closed as if recalling the long distant past, the story came out.

Her late husband had worked as a taxidermist in the Natural History department of Norwich Castle Museum. He also did taxidermy for private clients. The attic had been his workshop. Over the years, for his own pleasure and partly as an advertisement for his craft, he had built that diorama. The scene was based upon the view he had had from his boyhood bedroom at Horton-in-Ribblesdale.

That Cat!

Looking back I don't know how we managed it. At the time I am thinking of our family of three were teenagers. In addition there was Mungo, the setter, and two cats called Ginger and Blackie. I was the odd one out as all the rest were Yorkshire born: I was the off-comed 'un.

Ginger and Blackie came to us the way that cats so often do. The girls wanted a cat; we went to a local farm where they had a new litter and came away with two — both toms. Our elder daughter decided Blackie was hers and the younger took Ginger.

When it came to naming them we temporised, calling them Ginger and Blackie until we could agree upon something snappy like Dot and Carry (which was immediately rejected on account of them both being toms); Fish and Chips; Burke and Hare or any other combination of names. In the end they remained Ginger and Blackie; although my suggestion that we call the ginger one Blackie and the black one Ginger was howled down by shrill female voices.

Then misfortune and feline perversity took charge of the situation. Blackie was killed on the road and Ginger — always an awkward customer — transferred his affections to our elder daughter. He remained staunchly hers for the rest of his very long life. Ginger was a rebel, a fierce, loyal, magnificent monster who worshipped our daughter, terrified Mungo and maintained a cautious distance from every human who dared to set foot in the house.

I could write at length about Ginger but it would soon become tedious. Eventually the oft-repeated cry "that cat really will have to go" was on the point of being taken seriously. However, we settled into a guarded truce which became, over the years, total devotion.

There is, however, just one incident which shows that in spite of serious misgivings on my part, the old monster held me in some kind of esteem.

In those days we had a caravan with an awning. It was a perfect way to have a family holiday with my wife and the children sleeping in the caravan and myself in a mini-tent in the awning.

On the occasion I remember well, we went across to East Yorkshire — between Scarborough and Dalby Forest — for a week. Why we were stupid enough in the first place even to contemplate taking Ginger with us I cannot now remember. But we did!

It was a thoroughly incredible idea because Ginger hated cars. In fact, he'd hated cars ever since we took him to the vet to be castrated. In the end, after we had taken several short practice runs with the nearest thing I have ever seen to a flying fur-ball — a heavily armoured flying fur-ball — we settled for a doll's house shaped contraption and a suitable sedative.

We had sited the caravan and erected the awning before Ginger had fully come round. Not knowing what kind of mood he'd be in we left the opened box on its side in the awning and waited.

Ginger woke and stretched as cats do; first on his fore legs and then, flexing his backbone, on the rear. He stood and glared blearily around and tried out his claws. We all stood well back. But of fireworks there were none. He simply explored the awning and van and then decided that his chosen spot was to be on top of my sleeping bag folded onto the camp bed. The rest of the family got on with the job of unpacking and repacking. All this time Mungo had shown considerable restraint — my wife called it cowardice — and accompanied me strictly to heel. Whatever I did, wherever I went, Mungo was there.

Somewhere along the way Ginger disappeared. One moment we were aware of the baleful stare from those amber eyes; the next moment he was gone. We thought nothing of it until bedtime: no Ginger. Reassuring our daughter that cats do that kind of thing and quoting Rudyard Kipling as evidence — we went to sleep.

In the morning, still no Ginger. Our reassurances began to sound contrived and, in any case, fell upon deaf ears. That night more Kipling and further comforting words to a distraught daughter.

I woke up having dreamt that I was sharing Mungo's portable kennel; the cage he travelled in en route. In my semi-wakeful state he was clambering around. In my suddenly wakeful state I realised that Mungo was in his cage and that furry bodies were still squirming about me.

Ginger was trying to stuff a newly slain rabbit into my sleeping bag! Total wakefulness and chaos ensued. My daughter clasped her errant pet, my wife and other daughter expressed relief and went back to sleep. I tenderly laid the corpse of the rabbit under the van until daylight. Ginger broke free from my daughter's fond embrace and promptly came over to me to do battle for my sleeping bag. I won. Mungo, feeling jealous and slighted, turned his back on us all and sulked. Ginger prowled.

Next morning there were two slain rabbits under the van. They were removed but replaced by a third the next night. And so it went on. I was quite glad when we went home with family, Mungo and a somnolent cat drugged to the eyeballs.

We never repeated the experiment. There was, however, a corollary. Once home, Ginger transferred his affections to my daughter once more. He regularly roamed the countryside at night and returned at dawn via the open window of his mistress's ground floor bedroom. He always came bearing gifts.

Years after an animal psychologist told me that this was the highest honour Ginger could pay anyone. It proved, in fact, that he regarded the recipients of his gifts as his equals: well, almost.

Seasonal Snow

As I look out of my window it is snowing. Not furiously snowing; nothing approaching blizzard proportions. It is just a gentle and persistent fluttering down of flakes.

I love snow. As a child I welcomed it as a dog welcomes it: unconditionally. I didn't actually go out as Mungo did, cavorting around, leaping and trying to catch the flakes in my mouth. But I felt like doing it all the same. And what is more, almost all my favourite books have snow scenes. From childhood's snow episodes in Arthur Ransome's books, to the ending of James Joyce's story *The Dead* — quite a wide range of literary genre. I am captivated by snow.

The reality is just as gratifying as the literary. For one thing, it is possible to see which wild creatures have been where and done what overnight. Tracks of birds, from the delicate tread marks of sparrows and robins to the blatant paddle marks of wild geese, it is all there for the eyes to see. The invisible made visible by a carpet of white. It is surprising, too, how close foxes come to the dwellings and gratifying to learn that one's suspicions are true after all: there are badgers alive and well in the old sett in the wood.

All this enthusiasm has distracted me from the main point of the tale. To appreciate it to the full it must be said that frosty weather takes an annual toll, of birds like rooks which literally freeze to death and drop lifeless to the ground.

The year that I have in mind we had a fall of snow just before Christmas — the 23rd of December I think it was. By Christmas Eve, for once, everything Christmassy had been done. Even the preparation of the vegetables for next day's lunch. My wife, who had done most of the work as usual, sank thankfully into her chair before the fire. It was being allowed to die down before banking up and damping down for the night.

It was about 11.30p.m. I was feeling virtuous because I had carted and cut enough logs to last us for three days at least. Strangely enough I was wide awake. Now was my chance to prove — or disprove — an old legend.

At midnight on Christmas Eve, by ancient authority, animals are supposed to be given the powers of human speech. For a short time that is. I wrapped up warmly, told my wife what I intended to put to the test. Mungo must have understood human speech even if he didn't speak it because he was at the door ahead of me. The signs were good.

We did not do our usual route — across the paddock, down the lane, through the wood and back. At least, I did. Mungo, excited by the snow and the shadows cast by the almost full moon, galloped about, coming back to me every so often as if to urge me on faster.

As midnight approached we were far across the paddock on the edge of the wood. Mungo was investigating closely something unseen. Anticipating the church clock, which would infallibly signal the hour of midnight, I whistled up the dog. The ultimate test was upon me. He seemed reluctant to come but just as the clock began I saw him and his indigo shadow coming across the snow field to greet me.

He reached me, anticipating the first stroke of midnight. I crouched down to greet him. My heart pounded and I was trembling with anxiety and expectation.

Mungo raised his head and I stroked his ears. Our faces were close. He pushed forward; there was a gleam of teeth, a flash of tongue. He breathed against my cheek, his muzzle close to my ear.

Mungo belched: he had been investigating the corpses of the rooks at the edge of the wood. He wanted to share the experience with me.

A Yorkshire Gentleman

As I saw him come down the road I was shocked. Shocked by his almost prim manner of walking and by his apparent subservience to the woman who accompanied him. He looked, in fact, just as if he had come straight from some salon or beauty parlour. He, if indeed the creature was "he", was nothing like the Yorkshire terriers I knew and admired in my youth.

In those days the Yorkie was tiny but not minuscule; rough coated and at least as big as the smallest cocker spaniel. He was a man's dog, an inhabitant of the mill villages of the old West Riding. Along with the whippet and the racing pigeon the old style Yorkie was the third member of a triumvirate that had a place in even the poorest families.

Of course, being Yorkshire, he had to earn his keep. He was supreme at ratting, skilled at rabbiting and invaluable for flushing out ferrets that were earthed up. How are the mighty fallen indeed.

It is the old story, of course. A natural animal is taken up by the canine faddists and turned, by in-breeding, into a travesty: simply to feed the vanity of the so-called experts; the slaves to the Kennel Club and its arbitrary constraints.

But what about that other, notable, Pennine breed: the Airedale? Known alternatively in the early days as a Bingley Terrier, a Waterside Terrier or a Wharfedale Terrier, this breed resulted from crossing otterhounds with the basic black and tan terrier. The result? A unique dog: strong, bold and fearless and unshakably loyal to his family.

His size and boundless energy coupled with an insatiable appetite does not make him an easy pet but whatever favours are bestowed upon the Airedale will be repaid many times over.

As a guard dog (he was much used for this in World War one) he is the equal of the more exotic breeds imported from Europe. And both property and family are safe in his hands.

True Yorkshire folk will say that the Airedale exemplifies the essence of "Yorkshireness". Who am I to argue having been married to a true Tyke for nearly fifty years?

Do I have an opinion on the matter? On the outskirts of Huddersfield, going out towards Brighouse, there is a bungalow. A board by the front of the house warns intending visitors "Beware of the Dog". In a large compound around the back there is a stud of St Bernards: huge, leonine and loud voiced. They are safely housed.

But if you are incautious enough to go to the front door if it is only slightly ajar then watch your ankles. As ancient maps used to warn "Here there be Yorkies".

I rest my case.

ISIS publish a wide range of books in large print, from fiction to biography. Any suggestions for books you would like to see in large print or audio are always welcome. Please send to the Editorial Department at:

ISIS Publishing Ltd.
7 Centremead
Osney Mead
Oxford OX2 0ES
(01865) 250 333

A full list of titles is available free of charge from:
Ulverscroft Large Print Books

(UK)
The Green
Bradgate Road, Anstey
Leicester LE7 7FU
Tel: (0116) 236 4325

(Australia)
P.O Box 953
Crows Nest
NSW 1585
Tel: (02) 9436 2622

(USA)
1881 Ridge Road
P.O Box 1230, West Seneca,
N.Y. 14224-1230
Tel: (716) 674 4270

(Canada)
P.O Box 80038
Burlington
Ontario L7L 6B1
Tel: (905) 637 8734

(New Zealand)
P.O Box 456
Feilding
Tel: (06) 323 6828

Details of **ISIS** complete and unabridged audio books are also available from these offices. Alternatively, contact your local library for details of their collection of **ISIS** large print and unabridged audio books.

ALSO AVAILABLE . . .

Another Time, Another Place
William Woodrow

"Nostalgia is a disease of middle age and I should have taken precautions against it, but I succumbed."

With this gentle self-deprecation, William Woodrow introduces his charming memories of the Norfolk of his childhood and teens. In a series of engaging vignettes, he allows the reader to glimpse his early life in its many aspects. We see him among family, where he watches from the sidelines a matriarchal war over quince jam and learns from his grandfather to appreciate the beauty of nature, at play in the countryside fishing and boating on the Broads, and experiencing his first crushes.

The stories, however, are given unity by one factor: the author's intense and lasting love of the countryside. They are rich in the detail of local flora and fauna, dogs and horses are characterized with as much love as if they were family, and we learn of villages so tight-knit that a woman who married "outside" — even if this meant to a man in the next village along — would be ostracized forever.

Welsh Flannel
Derek Brock

Here is a completely fresh view of a small Welsh town, and the very ordinary people who live in it. Except that things seem to happen to them in the oddest fashion — like the trouble arising from Nancy-Boy Pugh's poor spelling, Trevor Evan's brilliant idea for curing baldness, and Luigi Evans' attempt to become the Tiger-Man, not to mention Idwal James's brave attempt to liberate a bunch of goldfish in Cardiff. The way in which the Welsh are regarded will never be the same.